ಜ಄

ART OF INVESTING

THINK LIKE AN INVESTOR
NOT AS A TRADER

ಜ಄

This page is intentionally left blank

*In Loving Memory of my brother & sister who passed away.
I look up to the sky and talk to you.
What I wouldn't give to hear you talk back.
I miss your voice, I miss your laughter, I miss Everything About You.*

This page is intentionally left blank

ART OF INVESTING
Sanjay Gupta

ISBN - 978-1-943851-39-3

First Edition, 2016
Copyright © 2016 Sanjay Gupta
All rights reserved

No part of this publication may be reproduced, stored in a retrieval system, or transmitted, in any form or by means electronic, mechanical, photocopying, or otherwise, without prior written permission of the Author.

Requests for permission should be addressed to info@dreamsanjay.com.

sources: https://www.google.co.in/search?q=antohny+robbins+pics&biw=1366&bih=643&tbm=isch&tbo=u&source=univ&sa=X&ved=0CCkQsARqFQoTCIOVmdmxm8gCFVUGjgod-KINxQ#imgrc=tRAoBAyzxI5UKM%3A

"Life will pay whatever price you ask of it."
— *TONY ROBBINS*

CONTENTS

PREFACE		7
CHAPTER 1	INTRODUCTION	13
CHAPTER 2	BEING STUCK	34
CHAPTER 3	INVESTMENT	40
CHAPTER 4	WHY S.I.P	51
CHAPTER 5	SHARES	61
CHAPTER 6	WHY BIG NO TO FUTURES AND OPTIONS	72
CHAPTER 7	THINK LIKE AN INVESTOR NOT AS A TRADER	80
CHAPTER 8	FOLLOW THE MASTERS	92
CHAPTER 9	BIRDS OF A FEATHER FLOCK TOGETHER	122
CHAPTER 10	GRATITUDE	128
CHAPTER 11	CONCLUSION	141

> "There is no friend as loyal as a book."
> — *ERNEST HEMINGWAY*

PREFACE

*T*his book will empower you to make better financial decisions; it will enable you to select the best mutual funds and shares.

In each chapter of this book you will discover something of value and learn how to invest in share market.

As much as possible, I have tried to share the information and knowledge I had used to grow my portfolio.

I would like you to go through all the 11 chapters and apply the same principles and strategies I had used.

In this book, I will share some of my experiences and the important lessons life has taught me, from time to time - Which factors were responsible for my repeated failures? After two deaths in my family and continuous humiliation in office and social life, what strategy did I use to get up, once again? And how I discovered my greatest strength i.e. INVESTING.

You will learn how to avoid the mistakes I have made, and why I have made.

By the time you complete reading all the 11 chapters, you will be a powerhouse of information, and in a position to advise the so called advisors (though you are not required to do that).

You will discover how to make better financial decisions and which tools to use for building a great portfolio, which will lead to the financial freedom that you have always wanted.

You will know and understand why, apart from helping you make better financial decisions, financial knowledge is necessary. I firmly believe that knowledge-> brings clarity of thought -> which brings confidence -> which brings financial freedom -> which brings a winning attitude -> which brings a blissful happy life -> which brings opulence.

I would like to thank the authors of the two great books which I read, again and again, when the going gets tough and when I start to doubt myself.

1. Think and Grow Rich - by Napoleon Hill

2. Rich Dad Poor Dad - by Robert Kiyosaki

My friends in America, who want to get an insight into the US stock exchange and are looking for a strategy to trade in the NYSE, can read a beautiful book written by **Tony Robbins**. I have read it completely. It is a really great book, with a variety of methods and strategies to use. I highly recommend that you purchase and read it thoroughly.

3. Money Master the Game: 7 Simple Steps to Financial Freedom – by Tony Robbins

My life is highly inspired by the words of Tony Robbins and Les Brown, so you will find that lot of words in my book reflect that.

I would also love to thank my beautiful daughter Naysa from whom I have learned so much. She has an extremely sharp memory and doesn't forget what she has learned.

For example, a few days ago I was playing a game similar to snakes and ladders with her. According to the game, if you win you advance certain places but if you lose or are in the wrong place, you are punished with fines etc.

I was winning over and over again, so after three games I told her that I was tired and didn't want to play further. To this, she replied, "Papa, a few years ago, you told me a story in which you explained that What **WINNING** means - It is not over until I win." So we played several rounds of the game and finally, in the seventh game, she won! It was only after that, she said, "Papa, I am tired. I'm going to play outdoor games with my friends."

I ask you - why don't we all develop this kind of attitude?

IT IS NOT OVER UNTIL I WIN

Folks, life is beautiful and you need to enjoy it. You don't need to spend your life in fulfilling other people's goals and dreams.

And you don't need to live your life in guilt and shame. You have everything you need within you. You just need to discover it.

Impossible is nothing. Even Impossible says - I M (am) POSSIBLE.

GOD BLESS YOU.

— SANJAY GUPTA

This page is intentionally left blank

ART OF INVESTING

THINK LIKE AN INVESTOR
NOT AS A TRADER

This page is intentionally left blank

CHAPTER 1

INTRODUCTION

I have been thinking of writing this book for a long time. Eventually, this book is meant to educate and empower you to apply your best knowledge to purchase Shares and Mutual Funds.

I got inspired by Prime Minister Narendra Modi's speeches. But I got the ultimate motivation to take massive action, while I was watching Dr. Subhash Chandra's show, where he shared stories of the common man working towards achieving big dreams. That's when I stood up and decided to take action, telling myself, "If they can do it, so can I."

Through this book, I am sharing and returning back to society the vast knowledge and understanding of the share market I have acquired over the years.

"To avoid criticism, say nothing, do nothing, be nothing."
— *Aristotle*

I had met people who started with nothing and accumulated lakhs (1 million = 10 lakhs) of rupees, then lost almost everything, and ended up where they started. So they got frustrated with the share market and blamed everybody except themselves for their failure.

These failures are in the habit of blaming everybody as an excuse. They were not able to sell on time because their boss had called, or some friend had come over, or wife had called, or there was an issue at home, or their child was not well. Even better, they would say, "Sanjay, you don't know, the problems in my home are different from yours," or, "My life is not as simple as it looks."

These people often say to me, "Sanjay, if the circumstances were okay, I would have made a big fortune." This makes me laugh. We can always come up with our own versions of a story, everybody does. But does that help? I tell you, if you have this tendency, resolve today that you will take full responsibility for your finances and will not blame anybody for anything.

Say the following lines 10 times in the morning after getting up from bed, and 10 times in the night before retiring to bed:

"I am 100 % responsible for any decision I make or act on."
— *Sanjay*

You have to give up complaining and blaming the circumstances. (When you are complaining, you are telling your subconscious mind that you want something but you don't have it. How can you become rich with such an attitude?) This is important. Do the above steps with belief and conviction. And do this exercise sincerely, with discipline, at least for the next 25 to 30 days. What will happen in the long run - it will tune your subconscious mind, and prepare it to believe that you are in control of your finances and you are responsible for all the decisions you make.

You may be thinking, at this point, that you have purchased this book to learn the up cycles and down cycles of the share market, and various triggers to sell shares. Don't worry. I will come to that too as you progress through the book. But first, I want to set your mind to receive the enormous wealth waiting for your claim.

Soon, you are going to discover that this book is not particularly about investment, mutual fund, shares, money etc., it is a mix of everything and my goal is to educate and empower you to make better financial decisions.

We all need money in our lives; **what matters most is whether you master money or it masters you**.

We all know we need to save more and invest more. So what is holding us back from taking action? Irrespective of whether we think we make good financial decisions or poor ones, we assume we are in control of the decisions we make. But most of the time, we struggle financially, which suggests we are not.

Good financial decisions bring financial security, independence, freedom and the time to enjoy the things that matter most. Basically, information without execution is poverty.

People often fail because they do the right thing at the wrong time. Ultimately, it's the right mix of right thing at the right time that makes you a winner.

"You can't manage your health if you can't measure it, and the same goes for your finances."

— *TONY ROBBINS*

The above are beautiful words by Tony Robbins. But how do you measure your finances? The answer is, through information. The more information you have, the more knowledgeable you become, which in turn brings confidence of making better financial decisions.

Remember, you will not make better financial decisions in a few days or months. However, you will develop the habit of making better financial decisions in the years to come. It is a Kaizen (continuous improvement) process. Have faith, you will get the confidence to make better financial decisions in a few years.

Better decision-making abilities will bring more riches, and more riches will bring you more **wealth**.

The whole idea is to convert your riches into true wealth, and for you to become *truly wealthy, the money needs to stay.*

For example, in the beginning of this book I had said, "I had met people who started with nothing and accumulated lakhs..." These people became rich through the share market at a certain time, but are not truly wealthy.

Wealthy people know how to make money and how to force it to stay with them, rich people only have money.

Once you know how to make money, then you can build sustainable wealth. The money never stops coming(like dividend income, share bonus, share splits etc.). If you have a reversal of fortune, it's not a big deal. You just make it back.

There are many examples in history of wealthy people who obtained their wealth through knowledge and valued knowledge more than money.

Wisdom and knowledge can create great wealth for anyone who desires it. As I had said earlier, wisdom and knowledge can be acquired with information.

The following are the sources of information that I have been using a lot:

1. Internet (google.com)
2. moneycontrol.com
3. Company's URL/company's website
4. CNBC TV18/CNBC Awaaz
5. Zee Business
6. Forbes magazine, especially Forbes India
7. Finance articles and more…

If you have correct and updated information and believe in your investment with a lot of faith, you will have great profits, provided you don't let everybody else's **FEAR** paralyze you.

Other people's opinions, views and fears, I call it **NOISE**. The best way to stop the noise and negative words from others is to ignore it. You can't stop others from talking, but you can change your attitude towards it. Also, you must discard or disagree with negative words as soon as they enter your mind because at that time, negative words are weak. Say to yourself, "**This is not true**." If you don't discard or disagree immediately, then the negative words will become stronger as they reside in your mind and it will become too difficult to uproot.

Let others say what makes them feel good, but you need to do what is right for you.

Have you heard about the ***90/10 Principle?***

I read about it on the internet. My friend sent a link across to me.

It will change your life or your attitude toward life. This is what it says:

10% of life is made up of what happens to you.

90% of life is decided by how you react…

What does this mean?

We really have **NO** control over 10% of what happens to us.

We cannot stop the car from breaking down.

The plane will be arriving late, which throws us off our schedule.

A driver may cut us off in the traffic.

We have NO control over this 10%.

The other 90% is different.

You determine the other 90%.

How…?

By your reaction.

You cannot control a red light.

However, you can control your reaction.

Do not let people fool you.

You can control how you react.

For example, let's say you are having breakfast with your family.

Your daughter knocks over a cup of tea onto your shirt.

You have no control over what has just happened.

What happens next will be determined by how you react.

You curse.

You scold your daughter harshly for knocking the cup over. She breaks into tears.

After scolding her, you turn to your wife and you criticize her for placing the cup too close to the edge of the table.

A short verbal battle follows. You storm upstairs and change your shirt. Back downstairs, you find your daughter has been too busy crying. She has not finished her breakfast and has not got ready for school.

She misses the bus.

Your spouse must leave immediately for work. So, you rush to the car and drive your daughter to school.

Because you are late, you drive at 70 km per hour. You have a small accident and a quarrel over it. After apologies, you drive away.

After a 15-minute delay, you arrive at the school. Your daughter runs inside without saying goodbye.

After arriving at the office 30 minutes late, you realize that you have forgotten your briefcase. Your day has started on a terrible note.

As it continues, it seems to get worse. You look forward to coming home. When you arrive home, you find a small cramp in your relationship with your wife and daughter.

Why?

Because of how you had reacted in the morning.

Why did you have a bad day?

A) The tea caused it

B) Your daughter caused it

C) The accident caused it

D) You caused it

The answer is D.

You had no control over what happened with the tea. How you reacted in those 5 seconds is what caused your bad day.

Here is what could have and should have happened.

Tea splashes over you. Your daughter is about to cry. You say to her gently, "It's okay. You just need to be more careful next time."

Grabbing a towel, you go upstairs and change your shirt. You grab your briefcase and come downstairs in time to look through the window and see your child getting on the bus. She turns and waves. You arrive 5 minutes early and the cheerful staff greets you. Did you notice the difference?

Two different scenarios, both of which started the same, ended different. Why?

Because of how you reacted.

You really had no control over 10% of what happened in your life. The other 90% was determined by your reaction.

Here are some ways to apply the 90/10 Principle in your life:

If someone says something negative about you, do not be a **sponge**. Let the attack roll off you like **water on glass**. You should not let the **negative comments** affect you. React properly, don't **ruin** your day.

A wrong reaction could result in losing a friend or getting stressed out.

How do you react if someone cuts you off in the traffic?

Do you lose your temper?

Pound on the steering wheel?

Shout and get into a road-rage?

Does your blood pressure skyrocket?

Who cares if you arrive **10 minutes** late at work?

Why let the cars ruin your drive?

Remember the 90/10 Principle and stop worrying about it.

You are told that you have lost your **job**. Why lose sleep and get irritated?

Use your worrying energy and your time to find a new job.

Do you know the best investments that will surely get you rich?

Wealth cannot be achieved by having a **high income alone**. What is the use of having a high income if nothing is left at the end of the month?

Focus on building wealth.

You can build wealth from nothing.

Wealth refers to the time or period that you can survive without working for money or taking help from other people. You can survive, provided you have savings and investments that can surely give you a passive income.

If you are wealthy, it means you do not have to worry about **tomorrow's expenses**. You can leave your job without bothering about your bills or how you can survive.

My personal advice to you is – first, invest in acquiring financial knowledge.

One of the great founding fathers of the United States, Benjamin Franklin, said, "An investment in knowledge pays the best interest."

The people who have ample knowledge of making money know the best investments to get rich. They have created a system or a business that provides cash flow.

However, it is not enough to have only knowledge.

Remember, knowledge becomes power when you put it to action. Successful people become wealthy because they are fearless in taking action.

Most people focus on too many things. They become distracted with material desire.

Poor people invest on the wrong things or make the wrong investments. They focus on spending on liabilities rather than on assets.

For those who don't know what 'liability' is, I will define it simply. A liability is a thing you invest in that doesn't have any returns, like all the money that goes out from your pocket from which you expect no profit.

I highly recommend that you read the book "**Rich Dad Poor dad**" at least twice. It will give you more knowledge than you can imagine. Write down and read aloud the following:

"Knowledge is Power."

— *Sanjay*

sources: https://www.google.co.in/search?q=antohny+robbins+pics&biw=1366&bih=643&tbm=isch&tbo=u&source=univ&sa=X&ved=0CCkQsARqFQoTCIOVmdmxm8gCFVUGjgod-KINxQ#tbm=isch&q=pursuit+of+-happiness&imgrc=MPVxn5wt5_w7uM%3A

The following lines are from **"PURSUIT OF HAPPYNESS,"** an American biographical film which stars *Will Smith* as *Chris Gardner* and Will's own son *Jaden* as *Christopher Junior*. It follows the story of Gardner and his son Christopher Jr., and their year long struggle with debt and even homelessness, as Gardner transitioned from a salesman of bone density scanner machines to a stockbroker.

I love this movie so much (It motivated me in the worst part of my life in 2008 when I constantly thought of suicide. This movie gave me the strength to get up!!!) that I have watched it more than 10 times, and some clips more than 50 times! If you have not watched it, then go ahead and watch it now. It's a must-watch for all.

sources: https://www.google.co.in/search?q=antohny+robbins+pics&biw=1366&bih=643&tbm=isch&tbo=u&source=univ&sa=X&ved=0CCkQsARqFQoTCIOVmdmxm8gCFVUGjgod-KINxQ#tbm=isch&q=Cris+Gardner+pics&imgrc=a6YU7r46xX8FDM%3A

Here are some of Chris Gardner's motivational words from the film:

Christopher Gardner: Hey. Don't ever let somebody tell you... you can't do something. Not even me. All right?

Christopher: All right.

Christopher Gardner: You got a dream... you gotta protect it. People can't do somethin' themselves, they wanna tell you, you can't do it. If you want somethin', go get it. Period.

I remember a time when nobody believed in me. But now, I'm about to prove them wrong.

It is nice to learn inspiring lessons from the lives of extraordinary people. Admiring the accomplishments of this once homeless father is not bad at all while building one's own career. Christopher Gardner rose from being homeless and underprivileged, into the most successful people in the world.

Though he was homeless and had a young son to take care of, Gardner did not let it stop him from realizing his dream. He became successful in his career - a licensed stockbroker, the top earner in his company.

Through all hardships, he built his own fortune and became a self-made **millionaire**.

At present, Gardner is a multi-millionaire investor, entrepreneur, stockbroker, author and motivational speaker. In spite of this, he is a very humble man.

Inspiring Lessons from Chris Gardner and how he became successful.

Let me share what I've learned from the successful homeless man and how to succeed like a millionaire.

1. Don't be Hopeless.

Being homeless or jobless doesn't mean that our life will stop.

It is a circumstance to measure how positive we are.

Sometimes we encounter trials to measure how determined we are to succeed in our dreams. It would be nice if we considered all trials and shortcomings in our life as challenges.

By not giving up and by focusing on our ambition, it is not impossible to reach our goal.

Gardner's ambition at that time was to get a lucrative job. He hoped to get a license to work as a stockbroker.

He never lost the hope for a **better life,** even though he had just a **high school diploma**. He believed that being a stockbroker would be the most rewarding job for him.

He kept working to reach his ambition. Being **underpaid** did not stop him from working as a trainee in Dean Witter Reynolds.

After the training program, he was hired as a stockbroker and a permanent employee in the company.

"We were homeless, we were not **hopeless**; there's a world of difference."

— *Chris Gardner*

2. Do What You Love to Do.

Having only a high school diploma did not stop Chris from applying for the training program for stockbrokers.

He had great **passion** for finance. Even though he knew that his income during the training program would be very low, he insisted on going for it. He became homeless due to his meagre income.

He became the top earner as a broker at Bear Stearns and Co. because of his passion towards his work. He became successful because of his deep desire to become a stockbroker.

If he had not pursued his love for finance, he might have still been stuck in his sales job, he might have still been going through a financial struggle.

In fact, Chris Gardner had given a piece of advice to Carmine Gallo, writer for Forbes Magazine, author, communication coach and speaker, which made a huge impact on his life and on the success of his business. This was Gardner's advice – *"Find something you love to do so much, you can't wait for the sun to rise to do it all over again."*

3. Work Hard to Reap the Rewards.

The main reason why we do not reach our goal is because we do not make enough effort. This is what I learned from the life of this former homeless man, who did unparalleled hard work as a stockbroker and an employee.

He went to work early and stayed back late in order to make 200 calls a day. He worked hard to reach as many prospective clients as he could.

He passed the licensing exam and became a stock broker.

His dedication and hard work finally paid off when he became the top earner in his company.

"Baby steps count, as long as you are going forward. You add them all up, and one day you look back and you'll be surprised at where you might get to."

— Chris Gardner

4. Overcome your own Fear.

Overcoming our own fear is somewhat getting courage to succeed in our **financial success**.

Chris Gardner left his sales job to attend a training program for brokers. He did not let his fear conquer him. He was determined and firmly believed that being a stockbroker was the most lucrative career that he could pursue.

In taking the decision to join the training program with a very low pay, he risked even the safety and well-being of his son.

Chris Gardner was not afraid of being homeless. He was not afraid of sleeping in the public toilet or in the subway station.

With his **meagre income**, he decided to be homeless so that he could afford food for his son and himself. And he determinedly believed that his being homeless was only temporary.

When the boss at Bear Stern's in San Francisco started noticing his performance, he began to receive a higher salary and more bonus. It was only then that he could afford to rent an apartment and a daycare for his son.

Chris Gardner is certainly a great example of someone who conquered his fear in order to succeed.

He knew that fear is the number one hindrance to success. Sometimes, we need to conquer the feeling of **security in our jobs**. We need to be determined to pursue the vocation that we dream about, either through freelance or by starting our own business.

You need to fight the fear of losing your permanent income in order to pursue freedom.

"When the circumstances that are out of our control cause us fear, tension and disappointment, it is human to feel those emotions, but they cannot defeat us."

— *Chris Gardner*

5. Mind Your Own Business.

Chris Gardner was not content to be the top earner in his company. His income from his employment was not sufficient and he desired more for his himself.

Gardner believed that he could create more wealth if he became an entrepreneur.

When he learned the ins and outs of the brokerage and investment business, he saw the bigger opportunity.

So, he **quit his job and built his own company**. He created a successful brokerage company named 'Christopher Gardner International Holdings.'

It did not prove him wrong. In fact, he made a lot of money from his own business.

What all these mega businesses of today have in common is that their owners dreamed big. They all wanted something, went after it, and got it, and didn't let anyone tell them otherwise.

> "**Don't listen to people. Dare to dream! Think big. Start small and work your way up. History is full of examples: Microsoft was started by two college dropouts in a garage. Today, it is one of the biggest corporations in the world, and a certain you-know-who is the richest man in the world! Apple, Google, Subway, Amazon, The Body Shop and HP are just a few other examples.**"
>
> — *Chris Gardner*

6. Sharing your Wealth and Helping those in need.

Sharing our wealth with others makes us wealthier. Giving to the needy heartily is like preparing ourselves to become more successful.

What you give to others will come back, doubly or more, to you in time.

Now I know that Gardner became a multi-millionaire because God blessed him with abundance and prosperity.

I learned that by NOT sharing our wealth with the needy, we are keeping our-selves small.

By giving like a tree, more leaves and buds will develop. We do not notice that our wealth grows abundantly like a plant grows lush.

When Gardner became successful, he did not forget the promise he had made to himself to help other people. He donated clothes, shoes and money to homeless families. Even now, he helps and gives training to homeless men and women to find jobs. He supports families to stay together and to get temporary shelter.

It is a sad thing that when most people become successful, they forget to help those in need. They become greedy and selfish.

We hear many real life stories of millionaires and billionaires who, after making huge sums of money and living in mansions, become penniless.

The main reason is greed of material things.

"I went to some very successful business people when I was trying to open the doors of my company, and none of them

would give me the time of day. I made a promise to myself and to God. I said, 'God, if you ever let me get to a certain level, I am not going to be like that.'"

— *Chris Gardner*

After beginning his career at Dean Witter, Chris Gardner went on to found the investment firm 'Gardner Rich' in 1987.

In 2006, Chris Gardner sold a minority stake in his brokerage firm in a multi-million dollar deal.

Chris Gardner is the living proof that in this world, it is not impossible to be a successful person. Being unfortunate and underprivileged are not obstacles in reaching for our ambition in life.

Financial success can be achieved if a person is armed with action, hard work, perseverance and determination.

With this, I come to the end of Chris Gardner's story. I will touch upon the power of giving in more detail in the chapter on Gratitude.

sources: mywealthdesire.com

You are one step away from taking massive action. Start small, but please take the first step. If I can do it, so can you.

GOD BLESS YOU.

CHAPTER 2

BEING STUCK

*E*verybody wants a better quality of life.

Everybody wants to be great at handling finances, but almost all of us get stuck at some point of time. Something stops us from taking the next step, and we become paralyzed and unable to take action.

How many times has this happened to you, when you have said to yourself, "*If only I had purchased that share or sold that share on that date and executed that order, my fortune would have been different and I would have ended up making huge profits.*"?

Everybody gets stuck at some point of time in their life and as a result we go through a lot of stress. It is normal. You are not alone or the odd one out.

Try to understand this - stress doesn't arise from **FACTS** but from the meaning we give to these facts. If you do not like the decision you have made in your life, change it. This is true of everything, not just finance.

If you don't like your portfolio, change it immediately. Do it now.

I manage my portfolio with ET PORTFOLIO. The link is:

http://etportfolio.economictimes.indiatimes.com

I am extremely grateful to ET for providing me with such a great tool. It has made my life much easier. Now I can have everything under a single umbrella and view my profit/loss on a single dashboard. This saves me a lot of time, which I can spend with my loved ones.

Once again, ET - thank you very much. Keep up the fantastic work!

This is what I have to say:

1. What you focus on is what you become. If you keep thinking, "I am bad at managing finances," you will be bad at managing finances. If you say, "I do not understand the share market," you will not understand the share market. If you keep telling yourself, "I always make a loss no matter what I do," you will definitely make a huge loss.

2. People are in the habit of finding **negative** meaning in facts. I often hear people say that, "The share market is not for me," or "Keeping on at my job is the only way for me," or "I can only earn money by working hard at my job." The truth is, people who work in the share market also work extremely hard. There is a misconception that **lazy or greedy people get involved with the share market**. That hard working and honest people don't have anything to do with it. Actually, people involved with the share market are usually very hard working and honest.

Some of the common fears that stop you are:

"If I invest, the stock market will crash."

"The economy is bad right now."

"It is not a good time to invest."

"If I stay invested, I will go broke."

"You can put money in the share market but you cannot take money out."

"Share markets always fall whenever I require money."

Even my wife tells me, "Your current net-worth of portfolio is because for the last 10 years, my salary and your salary have been going into the share market."

Grow up, Garima. Remember, I also have the following expenses:

- Bank Home Loan EMI
- Credit Cards Bills
- Other Utility Bills
- Shopping Expenses
- Car Petrol and Maintenance Charges
- Capital Expenditure like buying Cars, Jewellery etc.
- Children's Education Expenses
- Holiday Expenses
- Marriage and other Celebration Expenses
- And many more

I have seen that **it is becoming a fashion with people to blame and criticize things which are beyond their understanding.**

I usually say to myself, "*I don't care if the market crashes. If it does, I will re-align my portfolio and swap my shares with quality shares that have fallen.*"

Look at my statements and those of other people. Notice the difference. The circumstances are the same in both cases, but the meaning I give to our facts is what matters. I have always re-aligned my portfolio whenever there has been a correction of more than **5%** in a single day. It is not rocket science, but people often get stuck to their old portfolio.

3. What are you going to do next?

   How much profit do you want?

   What are your goals?

   What targets have you set?

   What is the expected return that you have in mind?

   Will you sell when the stock is up by 20% or by 100% from your purchase price?

   How long do you wish to hold this stock?

   What will you do with the profits and with the original invested amount?

   Make sure that you come up with answers to the above questions. If you do not have any set plans and goals, then **forget about making a profit from the stock market.** If you are not willing to invest your time in doing a minimum research before purchasing, then don't bother to shoot in the dark. You will definitely go nowhere and will be stuck in the same place. Keep doing whatever you are doing. The stock market is not for you.

Suppose someday, you discover that the company you invested in, is involved in a scam. What are you going to do? What meaning are you going to give it? Are you going to be depressed about the share you own and say, "***Why me?***" Or will you refuse to let this stress take control of you? Are you going to get stuck or will you move on?

The stock market does not guarantee that you are not going to have a loss. But the above steps will give you the strength to come up with solutions when you do.

What is the meaning you can give to the facts that will tell your subconscious mind that you are okay with this loss?

If you've had a loss, then accept it. Acknowledge it. Be truthful and honest with yourself. Then tell yourself, "*I am building a great portfolio and I will sell these shares at a great profit.*"

When you come up with new interpretations of facts, things change and you make great profits.

If you don't take the above mentioned steps in whatever you do, then your focus will shift to what you are **afraid to do**. As a result, you will end up **doing the things you don't like**, which will result in a lot of pain and disappointment. If you know what you are doing, you can easily manage your finances and can come up with a plan to achieve your goals.

You might be thinking, "Is this going to take time?" or "Is it going to take a lot of effort?" Yes, it is going to take a lot of time initially. But as time progresses, things will get better, and it will take lesser time and effort once you have mastered the process.

Knowledge brings you confidence and confidence brings you riches. Any skill can be learned. There is no skill on this planet that can't be learned and mastered. All it needs is time, the passion to learn, and persistence.

So, go ahead and take the first step. Don't worry about what your family, friends or relatives will say. Just take the first step.

"Distance doesn't matter. It is only the first step that is difficult."

— *Marie de Vichy-Chamrond*

4. Replace 'NOT' with a positive statement.

If you wish to say, "I will not sell any shares at a loss," replace it with a positive statement. Say, "*I will sell shares at a profit.*" Our subconscious mind does not understand '**NOT**.' It will interpret your statement as, "I will sell any shares at a loss." Develop a habit of saying and writing things in positive terms. Or else your subconscious mind will keep you small and stuck at the same place.

You will find this easy, not hard to do.

Before you read the next chapter, I want you to know that it conveys accurate information that might easily change your entire financial destiny.

"Whether you think you can, or you think you can't – you're right."

— *HENRY FORD*

GOD BLESS YOU.

CHAPTER 3

INVESTMENTS

*T*here are many forms of investments:

1. Real Estate - Property
2. Gold/Silver
3. Stock/Shares and Mutual Fund
4. Bank Fixed Deposit
5. Insurance (Not insurance linked Mutual Funds. This form of investment I consider extremely bad as it doesn't serve any purpose.)
6. Further Studies / Acquiring Professional Skill or Knowledge (the best form of investment is in yourself)
7. Long Term Bonds

Nothing is a bad or a good investment. People should invest as per their risk-taking capability.

As this book is about investment in Stock/Shares and Mutual Funds, I will talk only about that kind of investment.

Shares and Mutual Fund investment should not be less than **25%** of your net-worth. Which means that you should put about **25%** of your income into shares and Mutual Fund.

If you are below 25 years of age, you should have 100% exposure to equities. As we age, we can have the following investment strategy:

Age(Years)	Share investment	MF
Below 25	100%	0%
Below 30 but more than 25	80%	20%
Below 35 but more than 30	70%	30%
Below 40 but more than 35	65%	35%
Below 45 but more than 40	60%	40%
Below 50 but more than 45	55%	45%
Below 55 but more than 50	50%	50%
Below 60 but more than 55	35%	65%
Below 65 but more than 60	30%	70%
Below 70 but more than 65	20%	80%
Below 75 but more than 70	0%	100%

Above 75 years of age, there should be no investment in either shares or Mutual Funds. Bank FD is the safest in such cases.

I have been following the above strategy for the past 10 years with discipline. And it has worked for me, giving me great returns in both up and down market trends.

As I said before, if I can do it, so can you. Trust me - just follow the above strategy with discipline and faith, and you will be able to unlock the hidden treasure waiting for you.

Don't say and believe noise words like, "The share market is not for you." It is a beautiful place where big money can be made easily. All it needs is discipline and patience.

You can have a great life soon. Think about all the luxuries you can afford and acquire. You can make your dreams come true.

Thousands of people have achieved it in the past and thousands more will do so in the future. History is full of such examples. So, why can't you live the life that you are dreaming of?

"Would you like me to give you a formula for success? It's quite simple, really. Double your rate of failure. You're thinking of failure as the enemy of success. But it isn't at all... You can be discouraged by failure or you can learn from it. So go ahead and make mistakes. Make all you can. Because, remember that's where you'll find success. On the far side."

— *Thomas J. Watson, Founder of IBM*

If people say you are crazy, insane, mad (*pagal*), unrealistic, a fool etc., let them say it. Don't argue with them and don't waste your time replying to them. It is only the so called crazy, '*pagal*' people who end up doing something big. People who are 'realistic' and extra cautious, those who look for **guarantees** in life, are **driven by fear not love**. And these people are in the habit of saying, "*It looks impossible*," and remain stuck to wherever they are.

Growing an investment portfolio is like nurturing a child. You don't except him/her to be good at everything.

You help, protect, guide and learn from him/her. I often hear parents say, "I don't believe I said that or I did that. How could I have been so cruel to my child? Henceforth, I will be more respectful to my child or I will listen to him with more patience. I understand that he is in pain. I will console him. In the future, I will be a better parent."

But when it comes to your investments, you are very hard and tough. Let me give you an example:

I'm sure you never say, "My child is now in school but the moment he completes his college, he should become the CEO of a company."Or, "... he is going to become the president of this country."Or,"... he will start his own Microsoft or Google." Again, you never say, "I ride a motorcycle now, but my next purchase will be either a Bentley or a Jaguar." Or, "I don't have a watch, but I am going to purchase a Breitling watch soon."

Instead you say something like, "I now ride a motorcycle, but soon I am going to purchase an Alto. In a few years, I will purchase a sedan. However, I dream of owning a BMW. If someday I have the money, I will own a BMW."

You know the importance of baby steps and are ready to give time to your goals and dreams. So why don't you develop the same attitude towards your investments? Why do you have unrealistic expectations from your investments? I hear a lot of people say, "I am holding on to this investment for the last one year but it is not moving up. It would have been better if I had invested in a bank FD. At least, my money would have been safe there. I will sell this stock immediately."

The problem with this type of talk is that you are telling your subconscious mind that you are poor in managing investments, and you are happy with Bank FD returns.

There is nothing wrong with Bank FDs. However, sometimes, Bank FD returns are inadequate even to meet inflation, forget about realizing your goals and dreams.

In my office, people used to spend long hours comparing Bank FD returns. Once, someone said, "Sanjay, this Bank FD gives 0.15% more returns. This is the best. The other banks are cheating us." I quietly replied, "Look, are you over 60 now? Are you a senior citizen? If yes, then we can talk about Bank FDs."

Hearing this, the gentleman walked away. My friend, if you are reading this book, then please know – No one is cheating you. No one is harming you. And no bank is going to become rich with your investment of Rs. 50,000.

Such people are negative, critical, and complaining all the time. Get away from them. Disassociate from them. They drain your energy. Like the vampires in horror movies, they have bad stories to offload on you and suck your energy out.

I will talk in more detail about these guys in chapter 9.

My next question is, "***Do you really want to become rich?***" If yes, then:

what are your goals and dreams for this year?

What goals do you wish to achieve by 31st December, 2015?

What are your plans for the next 5 years? What will you do with your investments on 31st December, 2015?

Are you going to sell or buy more?

Which of your shares will you swap?

What will be the size of your investment by 2020?

Which shares do you want to hold on to till 2020?

These are the great questions. If you come up with the answers, they will bring you more riches than you can imagine.

People say, "I want to retain my current portfolio till 2020." In that case, why do they keep looking at the state of their investments, every day? Why do they panic at each market fall?

For example, if you purchased a share at Rs. 500 and now it is valued at Rs. 400, but it is a great share and you believe in that company and you had done your homework before purchasing that share, why then do you keep focusing on that share in 2015?

These questions will force you to change your focus. If you want to sell these shares in 2020, then why keep monitoring them in 2015?

I know these questions are painful, but changing your focus is very important. Or else, you will never be able to hold that share till 2020.

Here is an example from my own life. In the year 1995, I invested Rs. 50,000 in some shares. In the year 2010, the value of these shares was above 12 lakhs.

I have ICICI Bank shares purchased at Rs. 23 with a face value of Rs. 10, without the split. I have purchased UTI Bank shares (some 600 of them) at Rs. 69 (UTI Bank is now called AXIS Bank). It was also at the face value of Rs. 10 without split. And we enjoy great dividends for all these years. So what I am trying to tell you? Investing is not rocket science. Anyone can learn it. But you need the patience to hold on to your shares. I have made a great fortune by holding on to these shares, no matter what, by believing in these companies. (Though my father believes that I have done nothing extraordinary and that I am still managing Rs. 50,000 on his behalf, like any other employee or consultant would.)

I would like you to focus your attention on the **power of holding on to your investment**. Develop patience. It can reward you in many ways.

I feel very bad when I see people living in poverty. Being poor is not so bad but to have poverty thoughts is a really big **SIN**.

I have seen poverty from very close. Oh no, we were not poor. But I carried poverty thoughts for about 25 years.

First, I should clarify that I don't think it's a sin to be born poor. But it is a **sin** to think and stay that way. You are poor if you do any of the following activities:

1. Your kids go to their friends' house but their friends never come over to yours.

2. You lock your house and go out so that nobody can call you for a birthday party.

3. You know how hard it is to stop being poor.

4. You know that you have few options.

5. You construct your house or build your investment with borrowed money (not a bank loan).

6. You fight with someone you love because they want to watch something else on television.

7. You tell your kid to sit in the car so that you can save parking money.

8. You never have more than a quarter tank-full of fuel in your car and you drive to the fuel station with the emergency indicator blinking.

9. You borrow someone's vehicle and return it without fuelling it up.

10. You have a tendency to come up with an excuse for not going to a restaurant and when you do, you always order the cheapest item in the menu.

11. You live luxuriously on other people's money, but when it comes to spending your own, you are extra cautious.

These are the major indicators of living in poverty and pursuing poverty thoughts. Being poor is not a problem but having poverty thoughts is a large problem.

We are all blessed with so much. We need to return it back to society, and help the poor and underprivileged. Poverty thoughts is a really big SIN and the biggest obstacle to becoming wealthy.

"HATE POVERTY THOUGHTS"

— Sanjay

So, until and unless you remove these poverty thoughts, you can't be rich. This may sound tough, but it is true.

The following are some of the greatest motivational speakers. I like them and relate to every word they speak.

1. Tony Robbins
2. Les Brown
3. T.S. Madaan
4. Sandeep Maheshwari

My goal was to meet them.

What is your goal?

Don't leave your investment goals open. Stop reading this book now and set a date deadline. How much should your investments be worth by December 31, 2020, or by December 31, 2025? What are your short term and long term goals?

What additional investments do you have to make to reach this goal? Write down this goal in your wish list. This is important.

I do it regularly. It works like magic. Writing goals on a piece of paper and visualizing them daily will make that goal a reality.

I have seen many people earning six to seven figures every month, but still travelling by bus, when they can easily afford luxury taxi travel.

When I talk to them, they have all kinds of excuses. They say that we should not forget our roots, we should always be humble, or we should be down to earth, and many more things. They have all the time to justify their actions.

I am quite prepared to agree with them. However, if I ask them to donate 0.1% of what they earn to the poor, Will they ever be ready?

What do they do when they see someone extremely poor? Someone who can't even afford a single meal and is starving while they are having *brunches* and *dinches* on top of two large meals a day? To them, I would say, "My intention is not to hurt you. But seriously guys, Grow Up!"

A very good friend of mine had come home for tea. She was telling me about a few traits of her husband. She said, "My husband has developed all those traits which he hated in his father. He had disliked them so much as a child and he had promised never to have them."

So what happened in this case? Why did this man develop those very traits which he disliked so much?

Actually, if you want to remove some bad qualities, say 10 bad qualities, you will have to replace them with 10 good qualities. Find someone to appreciate. Even better, find 10 good qualities you like in your father. If you can't, then find 10 good qualities in your family and friends that you've always wanted to have.

For example, if you have a lawn in your garden, and one day you see weeds growing all over the place, you have two options:

1. Pluck all the weeds individually and repeat this exercise whenever you notice weeds among the grass.
2. Plant new grass in place of the weeds.

Which option seems better? You will choose option two – because you will not have to keep on plucking the weeds individually.

So, my friend's husband has to replace all his bad qualities with good qualities. If he doesn't, then it will be almost impossible for him to remove these unwanted qualities.

The same thing goes for your investments. Everything is related. If you have certain investments which are not working out and their projections do not look promising, then go ahead and sell them off. But I'd advise you to purchase the same amount of good investments. (I do a lot of bottom fishing and swapping.) Don't ever change investment LOB (line of business). For instance, if you have Mutual Funds which are not working out, don't swap them with shares or gold. Look for better investments in the same LOB – Mutual Funds.

GOD BLESS YOU.

CHAPTER 4

WHY S.I.P

SIP stands for Systematic Investment Plan for Mutual Funds.

Mutual Funds are specifically designed to pick quality shares and diversify investment portfolio fund.

Professional managers who ensure rigorous investment discipline manage these funds.

The fund managers are generally able to devote more time to monitor these funds then individuals can, and tend to react less to short term market falls.

Equity Mutual Funds in India have been relatively consistent in outperforming the broader stock market.

1. The cumulative annualized returns of Equity Mutual Funds over the last 10 years have been significantly higher than the Nifty.

2. Good Equity Mutual Funds have generally created wealth for investors over 10 years.

3. Equities have out-performed other investment classes over long-term in India as well as globally.

You can say 'Mutual Fund' is a company that pools money from many investors and invests the combined holdings in a single portfolio of securities that is professionally managed.

To manage risk, the fund manager attempts to diversify the fund's investment objective.

Funds generally invest in a variety of investments, including equity (shares), balanced funds, debt and liquid funds (money market instruments like certificate of deposit, treasury bills, commercial papers and term deposits).

Individual investors own shares of the fund, whereas the fund or the investment company owns the underlying investments chosen by the manager.

As the number of Mutual Funds has grown, some Mutual Funds have become increasingly complex and specialized, and employ complicated investment strategies.

Systematic Investment Plan (SIP) is a way to invest small amounts at regular intervals rather than investing a lump sum amount at one time.

The SIP route is one of the safest ways to invest in the share market. Here the investor is not trying to time the Up and Down trend of the stock market. Rather, he is trying to average the cost by investing at regular intervals.

You get more units when the market falls. However, when the markets rise, you get less number of units for your money. Over a period of time, the average cost of unit goes down.

Let's see what this means. Suppose, you have invested Rs. 12,000 in 2015. This could mean Rs. 1,000 in January, Rs. 1,000 in February and so on...

So now you have made a commitment to invest Rs. 1,000 per month. You can invest a minimum of Rs. 500, which is the minimum investment allowed in SIP.

You can now set multiple date selection, say the first on the 7th of every month and the next SIP on the 21st of every month. As markets can go up or down at any point of time, you are reducing the risk by investing on different dates.

Remember, you are not timing the market. Timing the market is extremely dangerous and should be avoided as nobody knows to what level the market will rise or fall.

Always remember to invest in Equity Mutual Funds. Other form of Mutual Funds can be ignored. I have not invested in Debt, Balanced or Fund of Fund and I won't recommend them. (I will talk separately about ELSS Mutual Funds which I love to invest in just for tax purposes, as there is a lock-in-period of 3 years.)

You should invest for a minimum 5-year period. If you can't invest for 5 years or more, SIP investment is not for you. It won't give you good returns and you will end up paying brokerage and exit load.

I recommend that you should not have more than 2 equity Mutual Funds in your portfolio.

Why? Let me explain to you.

It will be difficult to manage more funds. It takes a lot of your time and energy to manage each fund individually. Also, it will be difficult to track the performance of each fund house.

There was a time when I had 8 funds in my portfolio. It was a pretty diversified portfolio with a combination of large cap, mid cap, infrastructure fund, energy fund and small cap of different fund houses.

My best performing fund (HDFC), I invested through SIP between the year 2000 and 2008. After this, I stopped my SIP contributions as I had other financial commitments. My initial investment of Rs. 80,000 ($1,200 USD) grew to more than Rs. 3.5 lakhs. I took out Rs. 2.5 lakhs in 2012 and another Rs. 60,000 year 2015 in May. Rs. 40,000 still remains invested.

These returns far exceeded any expectations. I am of course not calculating the percentage of return over a period of time on investment.

My second best performing fund was IDFC where I invested about Rs. 10,000 in the year 2008. By 2015, the value grew to Rs. 25,000. The returns from this have not been very good, but it still Beat Bank FD returns.

My third and fourth Mutual Funds were able to save my principal which could not match bank saving account interest returns.

My other four funds, can you believe it, have given negative returns. My worst performing fund has given **-70%** returns. This means that my principal eroded by more than 70%. When I asked them why it performed so badly, they shamelessly said that the energy sector had not performed in all these years and mine was an energy diversified fund. I will not name it, but you can guess which mutual fund it was.

So, based on my years of investing experience, I will say - You should not have more than two Mutual Funds. You should not be excessively diversified, or accumulate funds because you want to diversify. And finally, what matters is, the money you are making out of it, and not how much diversified your portfolio is!

Review your portfolio once a year. Some people will advise you to review two or four times a year. But when you do this, you will end up paying brokerage and exit loads, which will not generate good returns for you.

I review on the 1st of January, every year. I have been doing this for many years. I have already finished my review for 2015. My next review is on the 1st of January, 2016.

Let us suppose, I need to invest Rs. 50,000 in a year through SIP Mutual Fund. There are 12 months in a year. So, Rs. 50,000/12 = Rs. 4,166 each month. Now I will divide this amount by two. So, I need to invest Rs. 4,166/2 = Rs. 2,083 with each fund house. Now, I further divide this amount by two, i.e. Rs. 1,041 to get multiple SIP dates (I usually follow multiple SIP dates: 01, 07, 20 and 25, every month).

For one fund, you can have the first SIP date on the 1st and the next on the 20th of each month. For the second fund, you can have the first SIP date on the 7th and the next on the 25th of the month.

The investment amount is the same for both funds. So, Rs.1041 x 2 (multiple SIP dates) x 2 (two funds) x 12 (12 SIP months in a year) = Rs. 49,968.

The Power of Compounding

The concept of compounding comes into picture when investment happens through SIP at regular intervals with longer time frames.

The power of compounding underlines the essence of making money work when you invest at an early age.

Let's take an example.

Retirement age = 60 years.

Age when you start investing	25 years	30 years
Monthly Contribution	5,000	5,000
Number of Years of Contribution	35	30
Total Amount Invested	21,00,000	18,00,000
Rate of Return	15%	15%
Corpus Built	7,33,85,901	3,46,16,398

If you look at the above calculation, you can see that a contribution of just Rs. 3,00,000 made in the first five years has a significant impact on overall wealth creation.

sources: http://www.thinkrupee.com

If you wish to avail tax benefits, then only you should invest in ELSS fund and that too through SIP. Do not rush to purchase a fund in March, just before the tax season. Take your time about it. There are certain ELSS funds that give good returns. However, I don't love them because you can't sell them for 3 years (the lock-in period). So, even if you find that a fund is not performing and you wish to change it, you cannot do it.

Tax benefit under section 80C, can be availed through SIP into ELSS, which is limited to a maximum investment of Rs. 1 lakh.

Follow the above strategy with discipline, and soon you will have a great fortune.

But how do you select the two Mutual Funds that you should invest in? I strongly believe in the **KISS** principle (Keep it Simple, Stupid).

How do I select the best Mutual Funds from among the countless ones out there? I always keep my Mutual Fund holding in dematerialized form. You can keep your funds in physical form as well, but I love to keep them in the dematerialized form so that I can check and visualize my funds in a single dashboard.

I keep my funds with ICICIDirect.com where I can create/view/cancel SIP online with a few clicks.

I have been using ICICIDirect.com for the last 10 years. Other such services may also be excellent but I have not used them, so I can't really judge them.

One thing I forgot to mention is that I am not related to HDFC or ICICIDirect.com in any way and I am not planning to be so in the future.

To select the best Mutual Fund, go to moneycontrol.com. Select the Mutual Fund tab. There you will see the *best funds to buy list*. Focus on the equity tab. Then look for 3-year returns. Please ignore 6-month and 1-year returns as they do not matter. Now select the fund with the highest return value. ELSS is also okay. Now select the second best fund from Diversified Equity, of course the one with the highest returns.

So now you are ready with the two best funds. Now go to Mutual Fund meter in the website.

Enter the fund name you have selected - in the *Enter scheme box of Mutual Fund meter*. You can select the fund from the drop down list.

The system will navigate to the next page with the fund name and results. Now focus on the following 2 things in the results. Ignore the rest.

1. CRISIL Mutual Fund rank (Ranking by CRISIL): It should be like this: "The scheme is ranked 1 in ELSS category by Crisil (for quarter ended Nov 1999) rank unchanged from last quarter. If you are already invested in this scheme, you may continue to stay invested."

2. It should be very good, which means very good performance in the category - Green. Just good performance is not acceptable. If the fund is not very good, then discard the fund and select the next.

This exercise is boring and takes a bit of time but it needs to be done. Take advantage of this beautiful tool that moneycontrol.com has created for us. You need to perform this step before investing every year.

Okay, now that you know how to select the best funds on your own, don't pay any fee amount to brokers or advisors.

Their knowledge is limited and they can't cross the limits set by the company where they work.

Knowledge is the key and confidence comes with knowledge. You should know more about Mutual Fund SIP than the advisors. Only then can you win. If you don't, you will be giving away your hard earned money to such advisors who focus on their commission and funds that don't work.

Brokers and advisors are not bad guys but they are driven by the commission they get. They are also often paralyzed by the company they work for. **So how can they have your best interest in mind?**

Now suppose, next year on the 1st of January, you discover that the fund you purchased is not giving you good returns or is not in the very good category on the Mutual Fund meter at moneycontrol.com. In such a case, sell the fund immediately and purchase something that fulfils these conditions.

SIP is not required. All you have to do: is to swap the amount invested in Mutual Fund.

"You can be young without money, but you can't be old without it."

— Tennessee Williams

The advantage with Mutual Fund SIP is this – if you don't want any exposure to equities/shares then you don't need to watch business channels like CNBC-TV18 or ZEE Business, or read business magazines. All you need to do is select the best Mutual Fund and stay invested in it. (Select the best Mutual Fund through moneycontrol.com MF meter. ICICIDirect.com also provides fund recommendations but don't forget to look through moneycontrol.com Mutual Fund meter before investing.)

If you have an investment horizon of 5 years or more, then why are you afraid of market falls? You should be okay and keep smiling.

Even if you see that the share market has fallen by 10% to 20% from its peak, please understand this, that it will soon recover its losses. Trust me.

You do not need to look at your fund value every month. You only need to check your fund value on the 1st of January. Just stay invested and relax.

If you follow the advice and strategies mentioned in this chapter, you are sure to make a huge fortune. There is absolutely no doubt about it!!!

GOD BLESS YOU.

CHAPTER 5

SHARES

Before you speak, listen.

Before you write, think.

Before you spend, earn.

Before you invest, investigate.

Before you criticize, wait.

Before you pray, forgive.

Before you quit, try.

Before you retire, save.

Before you die, give.

— *William Arthur Ward*

If you wish for long term growth in your investment, there is nothing better than shares.

Before you invest, investigate.

The quote above says that before you invest, you should investigate.

For example, when you go to a clothes store to buy a shirt for yourself, you take a few decisions before purchasing the shirt. Let me list down the decisions you make.

1. You select the stores that are giving offers and discounts. Or you may say, "I don't shop at discount stores."

2. You will look only at the brands of shirts you like.

3. You will look only for your preferred colours.

4. Once you are done with choosing the brand and colour, you will investigate further and look at cloth texture.

5. Next, you will ask for the right size, cost, discounts, offers etc.

6. You'll then go into the trial room, to try the shirt on. And finally, you'll ask your loved one, who is accompanying you, how the shirt looks on you.

When it comes to buying a shirt, most of us go through the above mentioned process. At least, I do.

But when it comes to shares, we don't go through similar investigations. At least majority (above 90%) of the people don't.

So, we know, the minimum time spent in purchasing the shirt is 30 minutes to an hour, or more. Parking and driving takes up some more time. And the shirt costs approximately between Rs. 1,000 to Rs. 2,000. However, for shares, which we buy for larger sums of money, we do not investigate at all. We get tips for shares over coffee tables in cafeterias. Some experts air their views about shares on business channels, over lunches and in social gatherings. Sometimes, friends and relatives provide advice. At other times, one hears people talking, in a public transport or some other place, about the potential of a share. People are in the habit of purchasing shares impulsively, depending on these tips. Then they keep hoping their shares will go up!

And once they own this share, they feel pretty smart about it.

Usually, people invest between Rs. 5,000 to Rs. 50,000 based on such tips. Personally, I have never invested so foolishly, not even twenty five years ago when I purchased my first share for my father. (For this wisdom, I thank God, as it is his gift to me.)

"Believe nothing, no matter where you read it, or who said it, no matter if I have said it, unless it agrees with your own reason and your own common sense."

— *Lord Buddha*

If you have purchased some shares because somebody said something about that company, and you have not done any **INVESTIGATION**, then you should know that this type of stock fishing is stupid and dangerous.

Let me explain you. You never buy a shirt or trouser just because a colleague, friend or relative has it.

But we always do this when it comes to stocks and shares. **Are we born lazy?** Not at all. What happens is this - when it comes to stock, we think that the other person is more intelligent than us and that he has probably done the required investigations.

So, we put our mind to rest and tell ourselves that no investigation is required. As I said, we are not born lazy. So how do you prepare your mind to investigate before you purchase shares?

Consider other people (including me) as fool, madmen and idiots. Think of yourself as very intelligent and smart about the share market. By doing this, you tell your subconscious mind that others are fools and you have more information and knowledge than them.

But you don't really, do you?

Well, you have to gather information and knowledge. And for that, you have to put your mind to work. So, you might say:

WORK -> MISSION -> FOCUS -> ENERGY -> KNOWLEDGE -> INFORMATION = INVESTIGATION

If you conduct your investigation in this manner, you can save a lot of the money that you pay to Tip advisors, fundamental specialists, experts and consultants.

You need to consider the following questions before you purchase any shares:

1. Why do you want to purchase this share?

2. Which sector does this company belong to (eg. pharmaceutical, finance, IT, manufacturing etc.)?

3. How long do you want to hold on to this share? Remember, this book is not for a trader but for a true investor.

4. What is the industry and company PE?

The price-to-earnings ratio, commonly known as the P/E ratio, is one of the most widely used valuation metrics.

It is a basic measure used to compare different investments or the same investment over different periods of time, and it's simple to calculate.

The P/E ratio is most commonly used for a quick comparison between two stocks to see how the stock market values them, with a higher P/E suggesting that future earnings are more likely.

Dividing the common stock market share price (numerator) by earnings per share (denominator) produces the ratio. For example, a stock with a market price of Rs. 100.00 and earnings of Rs. 10.00 per share would have a P/E ratio of 10(100/10=10).

P/E ratios can be calculated on past or realized earnings, projected earnings, or a combination of each.

Earnings are sometimes adjusted to exclude extraordinary events, since they are unlikely to repeat. When considering P/E ratios, it is important to understand if and how earnings have been adjusted and whether they are actual or projections.

sourceshttp: //www.moneycrashers.com/price-earnings-pe-ratio-definition-explained/

5. What is the future of the industry as a whole?

6. What are the government's plans for this industry? (This is especially important if the industry is dependent on government tenders like Railway stock.)

7. What are the future plans of the company?

8. Who are their competitors?

9. What is the company's past performance? (I always look at the company's performance for the last 5 years. If it is a new company, then one should check its performance since its inception, or at least for the last four quarters.)

10. What is the face value of the stock?

11. What is its dividend paying history? As this is great valuation question, so I would love to elaborate more here, I don't consider those companies good which don't declare any dividends at all.

Though this is not a criteria to reject any company but it is a important valuation factor, I generally give those companies a 10% valuation point which has a good dividend track report and has consistently declared dividends for the last 5 years.

12. When was the last split happened? And what was the ratio?

13. Most importantly – what percentage of net profit does this company make after interest and taxes?

14. Has this company issued any bonus shares? If it has - when?

15. What is the valuation of this company?

16. What is the total debt on this company and what does the company say about it?

17. Are there any litigation, pending orders, court cases, criminal cases, tax demand cases on this company and its directors?

18. Is there some good stock of a competitor available and what is its valuation, PE ratio, profits and dividends?

19. What does the website say about the company? (Here, I try to judge their presentation skills. If you can't sell yourself then how can you be a leader?)

20. What does the industry says about this company?

Is that a lot of things to do? I never said that money from stock can be generated quickly and without effort. It will require effort and time to investigate. You should be ready for it.

Look at the people who buy lottery tickets. What are the chances of their winning? The probability is extremely poor, sometimes as low as one in fourteen million. Even then, people keep on wasting their hard earned money on such foolish things.

For example, ten years ago, I was having a discussion with my friend. He'd purchased some shares for Rs. 50,000. I asked him a few questions (from the above questionnaire) about those shares. He became uncomfortable.

If you discuss money, it makes people feel bad. And people don't like to feel bad. So they simply stop talking about it. From that day, I promised myself that I would not give advice to anybody, especially on the subject of stock.

Since then, a lot of people have asked me about which stock to invest in or where to put their money. Generally, I never advise them. But now I say to you: Do your bare minimum homework before you purchase shares. A lot of study is not required for Mutual Funds (I have already covered Mutual Fund strategy in the SIP chapter), but for stocks you have to do the **investigation** as mentioned above. If you feel this is too much, then please invest only in Bank FD, not even in Mutual Funds as some investigation is required for that too. Read again the words of Lord Buddha.

Let me give you an example. In March, 2015, I selected Torrent Pharmaceuticals as it looked promising to me. At that time, the stock was quoted at Rs. 1,050. I did the investigation steps I mentioned, and I was through with the investigation by July, 2015. It took me almost five months to investigate. (You might say, "You are too slow in investigation." But actually, I had other commitments. Apart from investigating this stock, I was also investigating many other stocks.) By the time I was through with the investigation, this stock was quoting at Rs. 1,350. The stock price had gone up too fast, too quickly. So, I decided to drop this stock from my future stock list. "This stock can go up to Rs. 2000. I don't care," Before I began to write this chapter, this stock had gone up to Rs. 1,720 and now, on the 9th September, 2015, it is trading at Rs. 1,490, down 3.5% from its previous day closing.

You see, a majority of people enter the stock market with fear thoughts in their mind, hoping they don't lose their money. But statistics say that they do end up losing money. I have hundreds of stories on stocks. Let me tell you a few more…

I invested in **Indo Count Industries** as its story looked promising to me. After doing my investigation, I finally decided to purchase it. I bought at Rs. 700 in July, 2015. I generally never sell any share before making a profit of 50% or more. So, I decided to sell if the price went above Rs. 1,100. As I have to pay for brokerage and transaction tax, I keep the price a little higher. A few days later, my wife told me of the strategy that Arun's (CEO of the company where my wife works) wife follows - she generally sells with a profit of 20%, as the Indian share market is going through turmoil (due to the China factor). I thought this was a good idea. So, I decided to sell at a profit of 25% (as I needed to include brokerage and transaction tax charges). But the stock was already quoting at Rs. 1,000. Therefore, I decided to sell immediately. Once the sale order was executed, I decided to purchase this stock back at a 25% lower price, which came to Rs. 750 per share. As I had done my investigation at this price point, I decided to set the trigger at this cost. (I use a system for this, which I will tell you about in the next chapter.) Yesterday, I was able to purchase back this share at Rs. 750 and today, on the 9th September, 2015, the share is quoting at Rs. 830. (This, I think, was a miracle that worked in my favour. The moment the price of the stock went below Rs. 750, I received an SMS. I immediately purchased this share. In just a few minutes the price went up again, way above Rs. 800.)

Though I strongly believe in the long term stories and have purchased this stock for long term, Arun's wife's strategy can be applied when the market is in turmoil. And yes, making money makes me happy.

I have many more stories to share but I would like to conclude this chapter with just the above example, or else I might just go on and on.

I would like to tell you just one more thing - I consider **Initial Public Offering (IPO)** of stock a bad investment. Firstly because you block the full amount of your investment when you apply with no guarantee that you will get the full stock you applied for.

Secondly, it is almost impossible to predict whether the stock will list above the offer price. In most cases, you can get the stock on later dates at much below the offer price, and sometimes at 25% to 50% below the offer price. If you look at the IPOs of the past 5 years, you will know why I am saying this.

GOD BLESS YOU.

CHAPTER 6

WHY A BIG NO TO FUTURES AND OPTIONS

"Risk comes from not knowing what you're doing."
— *Warren Buffett*

Please don't trade with your money on Futures and Options (F&O). It is nothing but a form of gambling. (In fact it is the worst form of gambling that can be played on your laptop or on the Internet.)

The system is designed to make you lose money fast. Some 93% to 95% people lose money in F&O. It is like purchasing a lottery ticket and hoping that your number comes up. If you don't trade in F&O and lose money, how can the other **GREEDY** trader win?

I refer to it as a trade but analysts love to call it an investment (here one has to lose money so that others can win so trading their fears with peace which satisfies the other trader's greed.).

I strongly disagree with analysts and experts on this. Investments of less than 3 months (even if it is in mutual funds) are trades not investments.

If Call and Put ratios rise or fall because the Nifty is getting stronger or weaker, it may be fundamentally true and pleases analysts and experts. But this is happening only because one of the two emotions – fear or greed – is getting stronger.

The more fear rises, your Put ratio rises. The more greed gets stronger, the Call ratio rises. And both of these are the worst kinds of negative emotions.

Now, let me tell you my experience of F&O and the lessons learned from it.

I took a Tip advisor's services and spent some Rs. 50,000 on it. What a waste of money! I lost another Rs. 50,000 because of their advice.

A Tip advisor told me to purchase Nifty options at Rs. 102. But I was only able to purchase it at Rs. 109 as the price increased by the time my order was executed. He had also given a target price of Rs. 178. So, I was thinking of the profit I would make from this order. In less than 2 hours, I received another SMS from him saying that the call given at Rs. 102 was now Rs. 132. He told me to sell it. So I tried to sell. It was trading at Rs. 125. But my sell order was not executed. Therefore I went ahead and revised my sell order.

By now it was trading at Rs. 112. So, I put my sell order at Rs. 112. But its value kept falling fast and my heart was beating even faster. So I decided to sell at a market which was now at Rs. 95, and finally I was able to sell. My net loss therefore, was Rs. 109 - 95 = Rs. 14 per unit. So 500 Nifty units (20 Nifty lot) = loss of Rs. 7,000 (approx. $105 USD) in just 3 hours. The loss would be higher if we had included brokerage and share transaction taxes.

When the market closed I received another SMS from the advisor saying that I had made 30 Nifty points profit for a call given at Rs. 102 which sold at Rs. 132.

This is just one case. I can mention 10 such cases. I have experienced a lot of pain and anguish. So my advice is - never ever trade in F&O. However, some friends tell me, "F&O is good" or "I make money, so I will trade in F&O." Even then, I will say 'no' as the system is designed in such a way that you can win only if another loses. This theory doesn't suit me at all!

Nifty exchange is not going to fund your gains from its pocket. One man told me that this happens in everything. You are working in an IT job because somebody lost a job in the US. BJP won the elections because Congress lost. These negative, critical people are everywhere. If you want to **WIN,** then it is important to identify and throw these negative people out of your life immediately. The sooner you do it, the better.

Now, I will tell you another story of stock futures trade of 2000 shares. I received a call to purchase some company stock futures at Rs. 816 with a target of Rs. 823 and a stop-loss of Rs. 807.50. I purchased a single lot. I fixed the target price of Rs. 823 but the stock did not reach that price. At 2.45 PM, I received an SMS asking me to sell at Rs. 813.50.

I tried to sell at Rs. 813.50 but the price fell down further. Finally, my stop-loss got triggered, so I made a huge loss of Rs. 8.50 per share = 2000 x 8.50 = Rs. 17,000 (approx. $250 USD).

However, it did not take me more than 6 months to understand their tricks. The system is designed to make you lose. Also, options lose value of 5% each day, so Nifty of Rs. 100 becomes Rs. 95 the next day. Your Call/Put rises extremely slowly with Nifty's movement, but drops in value very fast.

One tip advisor claimed that they could double my money in 3 months. I was foolish enough to subscribe to their services.

If they are so good and can double your money, then why are they not advising the country's Finance Minister or the state's Chief Minister. They could eradicate poverty. In fact, by now, they should have eradicated poverty completely in the society they live in.

Tony Robbins, whom I consider the best motivational speaker on this earth, said, "Develop a habit of asking better questions." I go a step further. I say, "If you cannot get better answers, then focus on the next problem." Don't keep waiting for the better answers.

Here is a conversation between me and an F&O Tele-Caller:

F&O Tele-Caller: Am I talking to Sanjay?

Me: It's Sanjay here.

F&O Tele-Caller: I am _____ from _____. Thank you for your interest in F&O. From our data we have come to know that you are looking for F&O advisors.

Me: Yes, I am.

F&O Tele-Caller: With our advice, you can make a profit of 500 Nifty points or more.

Me: Is that true?

F&O Tele-Caller: Some people are earning Rs. 1,000,000 (approx. $15,000 USD) per month using our tips.

Me: By now, they must have become extremely rich.

F&O Tele-Caller: Yes, they are. They follow our advice.

Me: Which car do they come in?

F&O Tele-Caller: We don't know. We give services over SMS. You don't need to come to our office.

Me: Your company must be extremely rich. It must be registered in the BSE/NSE?

At this point the F&O Tele-Caller got frustrated and hung up.

Here is another example:

F&O Tele-Caller: Good morning, Sir.

Me: Good morning.

F&O Tele-Caller: Sir, we provide very good F&O advice. You will make a lot of money with our advice, both in Up and Down markets.

Me: Good.

F&O Tele-Caller: (She comes to the point immediately.) Once you have paid for the subscription, we will start the SMS services on your mobile.

Me: How much money have you invested?

F&O Tele-Caller: We are employees and employees are not allowed to trade on tips.

Me: Your father, mother, brother or someone else can invest on your company's tips.

F&O Tele-Caller: (Frustrated and angry) They don't like to trade.

Me: Okay, than why don't you leave your job and invest on the tips.

F&O Tele-Caller: My name is _____. In the future, if you want our services, you can call this number.

The Third Call:

F&O Tele-Caller: Good evening, Sir.

SANJAY: Good evening.

F&O Tele-Caller: Are you interested in Tip advisory services?

Me: Yes. I looked through your site and compared it with others. Others say that they will double my money in just three months. But your site doesn't say this.

F&O Tele-Caller: We are not frauds. Our tips are good, sure-shot. Our tips double your money in six months.

Me: In six months my Rs. 50,000 will become Rs. 100,000 and Rs. 200,000 in a year. Correct?

F&O Tele-Caller: Correct sir.

Me: Okay. I don't want Rs. 2 lakh. I will give you Rs. 50,000. You give me Rs. 1 lakh and keep the other 1 lakh. However, you will have to give it to me in writing on a stamp paper.

F&O Tele-Caller: No Sir, we are Tip advisors. You have to invest using our tips. We will not do it for you. You will have to take our subscription and invest on our tips.

Me: You don't want such big profits? Or does it mean that your tips don't work?

At this point, the F&O Tele-Caller laughed and disconnected the call.

The Fourth Call (The last one):

F&O Tele-Caller: Sir, are you looking for F&O advice?

Me: Yes, I am.

F&O Tele-Caller: We will provide you with Tip services on SMS. You need to subscribe to our services.

Me: That's great! Other Tip advisors also provide similar services. They say that we provide strict Stop Loss so that clients don't lose much money and make great profits. So, how are you different from them?

F&O Tele-Caller: We follow the same strategy as Rakesh Jhunjhunwala. We recommend on the basis of his strategies and principles.

Hearing this, I disconnected the call. He didn't even know that Rakesh Jhunjhunwala is the big **Bull** of the Indian stock market. He strongly believes in India's long term growth. And he advises us to stay invested, and not to sell in a panic. The Bull Run, according to him, will stay intact for many years to come.

These guys display his picture to advertise their product. If I thought, even for a minute, that this is true, I would ask these Tip providers, "Do you have Rakesh Jhunjhunwala's permission to use his picture to advertise your product? Is Rakesh Jhunjhunwala a shareholder in your company? Is Rakesh Jhunjhunwala the director or a partner in your company?" Actually, these people are very smart and they think everybody else is a fool. That is why I keep saying: **Knowledge is Power**. Increase your knowledge.

"A smart person will give you smart answers, but a wise person will ask you smart questions."

sources:http://www.searchquotes.com/

GOD BLESS YOU.

CHAPTER 7

THINK LIKE AN INVESTOR, NOT AS A TRADER

*L*et me begin this chapter with the following story:

Sir Roger Bannister was the first man to run a mile in under four minutes. Up until the time he did it in 1954, most people thought the four-minute mark was impossible to break. It was assumed that the human body couldn't physically go that fast. That it would collapse under the pressure.

People made the following assumptions:

- No one could run a mile in less than four minutes.
- It was impossible.
- You were crazy to even try.

That was, until Bannister proved everyone wrong. He achieved this by training in his own way, often for not very long as compared to his competitors, and believing that he could do it.

> "The man who can drive himself further once the effort gets painful will win."
>
> — *Roger Bannister*

So, what made people believe otherwise? How were they proved wrong? Usually, people say something is impossible when they imagine themselves doing it. So they express their opinion (which I call noise) by putting themselves in your shoes. What they truly mean to say is, *"If I was in your place, then I couldn't do it. It is impossible for me."* **SOMEONE'S OPINION OF YOU DOES NOT HAVE TO BECOME YOUR REALITY.**

Where your focus goes, your energy flows. Focus on what you want, where you are going, and what you are actively creating.

Give yourself the gift of experiencing at least three positive emotions every day -emotions such as appreciation, love, interest, amusement, joy, pride, hope and gratitude.

These emotions are powerful sculptors that broaden the landscape of possibility, expand your outlook, energize your relationships, calm your body, create emotional reserves and build mental resilience.

Focus, work and move towards a future full of possibility. Take massive action on your own behalf today to create your greatest life ever! You deserve it!

sources: http://impossiblehq.com/impossible-case-study-sir-roger-bannister/
The above quote is inspired from motivation speech of Les Brown

Understand that it is impossible for them, not for you. It is other people's limitations, not yours. Nowadays I often say, "I don't listen to these noises." But till 2008, I was actively doing so. For 25 years or more I was not doing the things I loved, because someday, somebody said it was impossible. And I considered it my reality. **You must get losers out of your life if you want to live your dreams.**

I was able to make myself financially free. In truth, I was ultimately able to experience true financial freedom because I stopped listening to such noises.

Many brokers and broking houses encourage you to trade in large volumes because it brings them more business -> more profits to the broking house they work for -> more commission for them. (Of course, what they earn is none of my business.)

Usually, in the BSE/NSE stock exchanges, there is an upper circuit limit of 5% for some stocks. It means that the stock can't go up or down for more than 5% in a day. For other stocks, it is a 10-20% circuit.

Now imagine that you are in an open position (which means that you have purchased stock) in the morning trade, and it was up by 1% when you purchased it, and this stock keeps going up till it becomes 3% higher by the middle of the day.

Your greed sets in. You tell your broker to square off the position (sell that stock) when the stock is up by 4% to 5%. This is because you can't hold this position, and don't wish to take delivery of this stock as you don't have the cash to take delivery. Also, delivery charges are high. Generally trading leverage/exposure which broking houses provide is high. You can trade more, i.e. purchase/sell with limited **CASH** on the same day. You can't hold the stock indefinitely. You have to cut/sell/square-off the current trade before 3.30 pm IST, before the BSE/NSE stock exchanges shut shop for the day. At 2.30

pm you check the stock and it is up by only 1.5%. So, now you begin to feel low, as you realise that you won't make much of a profit as you need to add brokerage at purchase and sell. At 3.00 pm the stock is up by only 1%. You get into a panic mode. Afraid that it will fall further, you decide to sell. But by the time the market closes, the stock closes at 3% up. You end up feeling terrible and really angry at yourself. Your day is ruined!

How many times has such stupidity happened to you? For me, it has happened many times. Even in cases where I have tried short selling (selling without actually owning stock), I have suffered losses.

Here is an example. I purchased some shares in the morning session (based on a Tip advisor's recommendations). As the advisor had given a target price that was higher by 3%, I was hoping to make a substantial profit. The stock got purchased at 0.5% below the CMP recommended price and I was feeling pretty lucky. However, the price went down by 1.8%, and the stop-loss got triggered. Thus, I made a huge loss.

8 out of 10 times, I made losses in my trades. But I learned my lesson quickly, in just two months. I made these stupid trades way back in 2010. In total, I made a loss (including brokerage charges + Tip advisor's fees) of Rs. 25,000 (some $350 USD).

Resolve that you will not pay these useless fees or be lured by the tricks and manipulations of brokers/share agents, who often have their own interests in mind. I am not saying they are wrong or they are cheats. But there are limitations and boundaries that they cannot cross. After all, they are faithful to their employers. They have to be. So they can never put your interest foremost.

I want you to **WIN**, not lose. I pray to **GOD** that you win in whatever you do. I am saying this over and over again - knowledge is power. So, increase your knowledge. Don't depend on Tip advisors and brokers. All you need to do is develop a **WINNING**

ATTITUDE. And knowledge is the only key. Don't say, "I can WIN." Say, "**I have to WIN.**" Leave nothing to chance or to luck. Dream of a wonderful life ahead and set the goals to achieve it.

People ask me, "Sanjay, you are so good at picking stocks. Considering India's long term potential, why don't you suggest some stocks that we could buy and hold on to?"

Firstly, I want to empower you, so that you can take the best decision based on your understanding and knowledge.

Secondly, I don't want to be another Tip advisor (I do not like Tip advisors. So how can I become one?).

Currently, I have some 40 stocks in my portfolio and based on my study and understanding, I consider 10 of them extremely solid. Also, their future projections look promising to me. I will give you the names of only 4 stocks. However, don't go ahead and purchase them just because I believe in their growth story. You too should have solid faith in these stocks. You need to have the knowledge, and must have completed all the necessary investigations that I talked earlier. Don't believe in a stock because I believe in it.

Confidence will come with knowledge, not with wishful thinking.

The four stocks are:

1. **IL and FS Investment Managers**
2. **Texmaco Infrastructure & Holdings**
3. **Multi Commodity Exchange of India**
4. **Edelweiss Financial Services**

Now let's talk of something else. You might have seen a lot of technical experts. Expert panels and advisors give a lot of useful information about companies, economy, stock market trends etc. And sometimes, they do give very good advice that works. What surprises me most is that almost all technical experts say, *"We don't have any position in the current stock, though our clients might have a position in this company."* This is the reason why they are always cool, calm, cheerful and smiling and can talk on any subject. Whether the market falls by 1000 points or rises by 1000 points, they are always composed. I was listening to an expert who said, "I said in April, 2015, that this market will not keep rising and therefore you need to sell. You will however get a lot of buying opportunities in August or September, 2015." What a vision! Yet these very guys don't invest heavily in the stock market. They only keep certain stocks in their portfolio for long term. **Why?** Because these guys want to be Happy and Peaceful, always. And don't want anything to compromise with.their peace, if things don't work according to their assumptions.

I recommend that you keep only good stock in your portfolio. There should not be even a single bad stock. Always remember, *'One Bad Fish Can Spoil the Whole Pond.'* If you can hold on for the next 5 years, then make sure you hold. The long term story of India is extremely positive. Make sure that you look at these long term investments when the country is having general elections, not before that. Otherwise you may experience a lot of pain when the stock market is in turmoil or your investments are going down. I have seen that people are in the habit of looking at long term stocks daily or monthly.

Now, what should people do when the stock market is in turmoil? How can they keep their minds in control? And how do they control their emotions in those trying times? Well, I follow this strategy:

I prepare and revisit the following list, and then take a look at myself. Have I achieved any of the goals? What do I need to do to achieve the next important goal?

100 THINGS TO DO BEFORE YOU DIE.

I can guarantee that you won't have your investments in this list. What happens is that preparing this list changes your focus, from the stock market that is in turmoil to the 100 things to do before you die.

The next thing I often do is think of and visualize a vacation or holiday trip. Currently, I am thinking of my Amritsar, Punjab trip. The points I think about are the following:

1. On which month should I go on the trip?

2. How long should the trip be?

3. What are the places that I should visit?

4. Where would I eat?

5. Where can I find the best street food?

6. Which 5-star hotel shall I stay in and what are its customer reviews?

By doing these exercises, you will keep your mind extremely busy. You won't have a minute free to look at the state of the stock market. Sometimes, I get so busy that I forget to have lunch or to talk to my wife. Make yourself busy, keep yourself preoccupied with these things, so that you don't have a single minute to talk to anyone. Forget about looking at the stock you own.

You may say, "That you mean that I should not look at the stock market? Then, how can I purchase the shares I wish to own?" The answer is - we have such excellent systems available now that we don't need to do that. For the last 10 years, I've been using **ICICI Direct**. Here, I keep all the stock and Mutual Funds. It automatically transfers funds from my bank account. I don't need to do anything. (I have a bank account with ICICI Bank and it is linked to my ICICI Direct account. I don't know how this works with other banks.) Their portfolio service is excellent. You can easily see profit/loss coming in equities. I have a portfolio for mutual fund operations as well. It is very easy to understand their order and trade book. (Please Note that, I am not related to ICICI Direct or planning to get involved with them. My opinion is based only on my experience.)

I don't know anything about the systems other broking houses use. They might have better systems then this, but sorry friends, I can't comment on them.

The ICICI Direct SMS service is excellent. (This, I love the most. It has given me a lot of peace.) You can customize/set a trigger for the stock you wish to purchase/sell. What happens is quite simple: I set the trigger on certain level. If that trigger gets executed, I get an SMS saying that the stock has crossed that particular level, and that currently it is at so and so price. At this point, I log in to my ICICI Direct account and purchase/sell that share (According to whatever I want to do), and close that site. It means that I don't have to keep looking at the stock market. I can spend more time with my loved ones, or I can do the things that I love.

Once, I felt that the brokerage at ICICI Direct was too high as compared to other broking houses. So, I called my ICICI Direct Relationship Manager and explained my concern. He told me about prepaid brokerage plans that I could opt for. Therefore, I opted for the prepaid brokerage plan and ended up saving 65-70% on brokerage.

ICICI Direct has introduced a new feature - VTC. It is very good and I use it a lot. What happens is - the system places orders for the next 45 days and you don't even need to log in and check what happened to your order.

Order Validity: DAY IOC VTC

Select VTC order in this case.

What is 'VTC'?

Valid Till Cancel (VTC) is a brand new facility offered through ICICIDirect.com. You can use this to place Buy and Sell Limit orders in scripts of your choice, specifying the period for which you want the order instruction to be valid. The period selected by you should be within the maximum validity date defined by ICICI Securities Ltd. (I-Sec).

How does VTC order feature work?

When you place a VTC order, you give an order instruction to I-Sec stating that if the order is not executed for the entire quantity, I-Sec is authorized to place fresh orders for the unexecuted quantity in your account on the subsequent trading days till the entire quantity is executed or till the validity expires, whichever is earlier. The feature allows you to specify the number of days during which you wish to place the orders.

Your VTC order will remain valid but will expire at the end of every trade date if the order remains unexecuted and if it is not cancelled or rejected. At the end of the day, after market hours, I-Sec will place overnight orders on your behalf at the same limit price and for the unexecuted quantity for the next trade date, provided your validity date is less than or equal to the next trade date.

URL https://secure.icicidirect.com/IDirectTrading/customer/login.aspx

I mean to say here that the systems are in place. Some of them are excellent system and you just need to have the knowledge. Don't keep on doing old things in traditional ways because you don't know the new system. Lack of knowledge is not an excuse. People don't know about something, they end up criticizing the system, which is not fair. It doesn't matter which system you use or how much loss you have made and when. You just need to start doing the right things, after you have gained knowledge.

"You have to learn the rules of the game, and then you have to play better than anyone else."

— ALBERT EINSTEIN

Usually, technical experts and expert panels ask you to 'always diversify,' to have exposure to different sectors/business. Here are some of the clichés you will hear:

1. Don't put all your eggs in one basket.

2. Don't concentrate all your prospects or resources in one thing or place. You could lose everything.

3. Save more. Diversify your portfolio to reap gains.

I strongly disagree with the above statements. Why should you diversify? To avoid losing money, right? Look, if you want to play too safe, and your **GOAL** is to save the principal, then the stock market is not for you. Better invest in Bank FDs. To be very frank, share market investment is a risky proposition. But over a long term period, you will gain heavily, not just double but triple your investment. Some stocks can go even upto 10 to 20 times their original Value. Diversification does not guarantee that your principal will be 100% safe. You will lose, but you will not lose heavily. If the market goes down, your portfolio will be saved. But there are no guarantees. After all, you are trying to put a few eggs in many baskets, right?

Think. If instead, you had taken the strategy of putting many eggs in a few baskets, in sectors that were buzzing (you would know which ones as you would have selected the stocks after doing the necessary investigations and research), then some of your stocks might have exploded like anything, and some might have gone up even more than 50 times. (Some 15 years ago, I had invested heavily in the banking sector. And banking stocks returns exploded, giving more than 40-80 times returns, once even 100 times returns.) So, if you have done all the investigations and **are not gambling with stocks**, then your chances of losing are extremely slim. If you are open to risk, then take 100% risk. Don't play too safe. Who knows, you may have exposure to that sector which is ready to explode.

GOD BLESS YOU.

CHAPTER 8

FOLLOW THE MASTERS

From my previous chapters or subsequent chapters, you can easily figure out that I, In general, don't like advisors/experts. They only know a few things but can give you advice on everything. And most of the time, their lives are in a mess. But there are exceptions to this.

A few of these advisors/experts have accumulated large amounts of wealth with their vast knowledge and experience.

"**When a person with money meets a person with experience, the person with the experience winds up with the money, and the person with the money winds up with the experience.**"
— *Harvey MacKay*

Warren Buffett

Source: https://www.google.co.in/search?q=antohny+robbins+pics&biw
=1366&bih=643&tbm=isch&tbo=u&source=univ&sa=X&ved=0CCkQsA
RqFQoTCIOVmdmxm8gCFVUGjgod-KINxQ#tbm=isch&q=Warren+Buffett
+pics&imgdii=JOrE4si7H2g22M%3A%3BJOrE4si7H2g22M%3A%3By_
28yiAoBPdS6M%3A&imgrc=JOrE4si7H2g22M%3A

Known as the 'Oracle of Omaha,' Warren Buffett is an investment guru and one of the richest and most respected businessmen in the world.

Biography

Born in Nebraska in 1930, Warren Buffett demonstrated keen business abilities at a young age. He formed the Buffett Partnership Ltd. in 1956, and by 1965 he had assumed control of Berkshire Hathaway. Overseeing the growth of a conglomerate with holdings in the media, insurance, energy, and food and beverage industries, Buffett became one of the world's richest men and a celebrated philanthropist.

Early Life

Businessman and investor, Warren Edward Buffett, was born on 30th August, 1930, in Omaha, Nebraska. Buffett's father, Howard, worked as a stockbroker and served as a U.S. Congressman. His mother, Leila Stahl Buffett, was a homemaker. Warren Buffett was the second of three children and the only son.

Warren Buffett demonstrated a knack for financial and business matters early in his childhood. Friends and acquaintances have said that the young boy was a mathematical prodigy who could add large columns of numbers in his head, a talent he occasionally demonstrated in his later years.

Warren Buffett often visited his father's stock-brokerage shop as a child, and chalked out the stock prices on the blackboard in the office. At the age of 11, he made his first investment, buying three shares of Cities Service preferred at $38 per share.

The stock quickly dropped to only $27, but Warren Buffett held on tenaciously until they reached $40. He sold his shares at a small profit, but regretted the decision when Cities Service shot up to nearly $200 a share. He later cited this experience as an early lesson in **patience in investing**.

First Entrepreneurial Venture

By the age of 13, Buffett was running his own business as a paperboy, and also selling his own horseracing tip sheet. That same year, he filed his first tax return, claiming a $35 tax deduction for his bike.

In 1942, Warren Buffett's father was elected to the U.S. House of Representatives, and his family moved to Fredericksburg in Virginia to be closer to the congressman's new post.

Warren Buffett attended the Woodrow Wilson High School in Washington, D.C., where he continued plotting new ways to make money. During his high school tenure, he and a friend purchased a used pinball machine for $25. They installed it in a barbershop, and within a few months the profits enabled them to buy more machines. Warren Buffett owned machines in three different locations before he sold the business for $1,200.

Higher Education and Early Career

Buffett enrolled at the University of Pennsylvania at the age of 16 to study business. He stayed there for two years, moved to the University of Nebraska to finish his degree, and emerged from college at the age of 20 with nearly $10,000 from his childhood businesses.

Influenced by Benjamin Graham's book 'The Intelligent Investor' written in 1949, Buffett enrolled at Columbia Business School to study under the acclaimed economist and investor.

After acquiring his master's degree in 1951, he sold securities for 'Buffett-Falk & Company' for three years and then worked for his mentor for two years as an analyst at 'Graham-Newman Corp.'

In 1956, Warren Buffett formed the firm 'Buffett Partnership Ltd.' in his hometown of Omaha. Utilizing the techniques learned from Graham, he was successful in identifying undervalued companies and became a millionaire.

One such enterprise Warren Buffett valued was a textile company named 'Berkshire Hathaway'. He began accumulating stock in the early 1960s, and by 1965 he had assumed control of the company.

Business Empire

Despite the success of Buffett Partnership, its founder dissolved the firm in 1969 to focus on the development of Berkshire Hathaway. He phased out its textile manufacturing division and instead expanded the company by buying assets in media (The Washington Post), insurance (GEICO) and oil (Exxon). Immensely successful, the 'Oracle of Omaha' even managed to spin seemingly poor investments into gold, most notably with his purchase of the scandal-plagued 'Salomon Brothers' in 1987.

Following Berkshire Hathaway's significant investment in Coca-Cola, Buffett became the director of the company from 1989 until 2006. He has also served as Director of Citigroup Global Markets Holdings, Graham Holdings Company and The Gillette Company.

Recent Activity and Philanthropy

In June 2006, Buffett made an announcement that he would be giving his **entire fortune away to charity**, committing 85% of it to the Bill and Melinda Gates Foundation. This donation became the largest act of charitable giving in the history of the United States. In 2010, Buffett and Gates announced they had formed 'The Giving Pledge' campaign to recruit more wealthy individuals for philanthropic causes.

In 2012, Warren Buffett disclosed that he had been diagnosed with prostate cancer. He began undergoing radiation treatment in July, and successfully completed his treatment in November.

The health scare did little to slow the octogenarian, who annually ranks near the top in the Forbes World Billionaires list. In February 2013, Buffett purchased 'H. J. Heinz' with private equity group '3G Capital' for $28 billion. Later additions to the Berkshire Hathaway stable include battery maker Duracell and Kraft Foods Group, which merged with Heinz in 2015 to form the third-largest food and beverage company in North America.

sources: http://www.biography.com/people/warren-buffett-9230729

What makes Warren Buffett a great investor? Intelligence or Discipline?

I thought this excerpt from Warren Buffett's 2011 interview in India was relevant to not only investing but also decision-making.

A member of the audience said to Buffett: "As we all know, you are an extremely intelligent person. At the same time, you are very disciplined with your investing approach. What makes Warren Buffett a great investor? Is it the intelligence or the discipline?"

This was Warren's response:

Warren: The good news I can tell you is that to be a great investor you don't have to have a terrific IQ.

If you are in the investment business and have an IQ of 160, sell 30 points to someone else... You do have to have an emotional stability and an inner peace about your decisions. It is a game where you are bombarded by minute-by-minute opinions.

It's not a complicated game. It's simple, but it's not easy.

You have to have an emotional stability.

You need to be able to look at the facts about a business, about an industry, and evaluate a business unaffected by what other people think. That is very difficult for most people.

Most people have, sometimes, a herd mentality which can, under certain circumstances, develop into delusional behaviour.

You saw that in the Internet craze and so on. I'm sure everybody in this room has the intelligence to do extremely well in investments.

Moderator: They're all 160 IQs.

Warren: They don't need it. I'm disappointed they haven't sold off some already. The 160s won't beat the 130s at all necessarily. They may, but they do not have a big edge. The ones that have the edge are the ones who really have the temperament to look at a business, look at an industry and not care what the person next to them thinks about it, not care what they read about it in the newspaper, not care what they hear about it on the television, not listen to people who say, "This is going to happen," or, "That's going to happen."

You have to come to your own conclusions, and you have to do it based on facts that are available. If you don't have enough facts to reach a conclusion, you forget it. You go on to the next one. You have to also have the willingness to walk away from things that other people think are very simple.

A lot of people don't have that. I don't know why it is. I've been asked a lot of times whether that was something that you're born with or something you learn. I'm not sure I know the answer. Temperament's important.

Moderator: That's very good advice, to be detached from all the noise. You shouldn't go with the herd.

Warren: If you don't know the answer yourself don't expect somebody else to tell you. If you don't know the answer yourself and somebody else says they know the answer, don't let that fact push you into coming to a conclusion about something that you don't know enough to come to a conclusion on.

Stocks go up and down, there is no game where the odds are in your favour. But to win at this game, and most people can't, you need discipline to form your own opinions and the right temperament, which is more important than IQ.

Pascal said it best: "All men's miseries derive from not being able to sit in a quiet room alone."

Warren: If you look at the typical stock on the New York Stock Exchange, its high will be, perhaps, for the last 12 months will be 150 percent of its low so they're bobbing all over the place. All you have to do is sit there and wait until something is really attractive that you understand.

And you can forget about everything else. That is a wonderful game to play in. There's almost nothing where the game is stacked in your favour like the stock market.

What happens is people start listening to everybody talk on television or whatever it may be or read the paper, and they take what is a fundamental advantage and turn it into a disadvantage. There's **no easier game than stocks**. You have to be sure you **don't play it too often.**

You need the discipline to say no.

Ajit Jain (A Senior Executive at Berkshire Hathaway): The discipline to say no, if you have that and you're not willing to let people steamroll you into saying yes. If you have that discipline, that's more than 50 percent of the battle.

Warren: Don't do anything in life where, if somebody asks you the reason why you are doing it, the answer is "Everybody else is doing it." I mean, if you cancel that as a rationale for doing an activity in life, you'll live a better life whether it's in the stock market or any place else.

I've seen more dumb things, and sometimes even illegal things, justified (rationalized) on the basis of "Everybody else is doing it." **You don't need to do what everybody else is doing**. It's maddening, during the Internet craze when the bubble was going on.

Here's your neighbour who's got an IQ of 50 points below you, and he's making all this easy money and your wife is telling you "This jerk next door is making money, and you're smarter than he is. Why aren't you making money?"

You have to forget about all those things, you have to do what works, what you understand, and if you don't understand it and somebody else is doing it, don't get envious or anything of the sort.

Just go on and wait until you find something you understand.

sources:https://www.farnamstreetblog.com/2014/08/what-makes-warren-buffett-a-great-investor/

Ajay Piramal

sources:http://www.thehindubusinessline.com/companies/piramal-health-to-pay-rs-3400-cr-for-us-co-decision-resources/article3424610.ece

Ajay Piramal's favourite story is "Footprints on the sands of time."

The story goes like this:

One night a man had a dream.

He dreamed that he was walking along the beach with the Lord.

Across the sky flashed scenes from his life.

For each scene he noticed two sets of footprints in the sand: one belonging to him, and the other to the Lord.

When the last scene of his life flashed before him, he looked back at the footprints in the sand.

He noticed that many times along the path of his life there was only one set of footprints.

He also noticed that it happened at the very lowest and saddest times in his life.

This really bothered him and he questioned the Lord about it:

"Lord, you said that once I decided to follow you, you'd walk with me all the way.

But I have noticed that during the most troublesome times in my life, there is only one set of footprints.

I don't understand why when I needed you most you would leave me."

The Lord replied:

"My son, my precious child, I love you and I would never leave you.

During your times of trial and suffering, when you see only one set of footprints, it was then that I carried you."

The story, Piramal says, acted as a guiding spirit for him. He was 29 when his father died suddenly in New York. His brother, Ashok, took over but five years later, he too died of cancer, leaving behind his young widow, Urvi, with three children aged less than 10 years.

Just before that, his other brother, Dilip, had decided to separate his share of the business. Meanwhile, a year-long textile strike led by Datta Samant dealt a crippling blow to the textile industry, and Morarjee Mills, the group's main business venture then, was deep in the red. **"Life looked bleak when I became chairman of the group at the age of 29. But I survived as the Lord must have carried me when I needed Him the most,"** says Piramal.

Going by his track record, there is hardly any doubt about that. From owning what was then an almost defunct textile company, Piramal is today the chairman of a Rs 4,000-crore (Rs. 40 billion) group, comprising Nicholas Piramal (the fourth-largest pharmaceutical company in India), Morarjee Weaving and Spinning, and Gujarat Glass. Piramal is also the chairman of the group's retail operations, which are now looked after by his nephew.

Each of his three nephews (Urvi Piramal's sons) is now in independent charge of a separate business. He felt deeply hurt by what he calls 'sensational reports' in sections of the media about differences between him and his sister-in-law Urvi, and his nephews' over-control of the businesses.

"As their uncle, I did my duty by holding their hands in the formative stages of their life. Now they are independent but we are all part of a big family. The story '**Footprints**' applies to me as much as it does to my nephews and my own children, Nandini and Anand," says Piramal.

On his 10th floor office at Nicholas Piramal Towers in Mumbai's Peninsula Corporate Park, the influence of the Lord is omnipresent. The walls have inscriptions from the **Bhagavad Gita**. The Bhagavad Gita is one of the greatest management books, as it prescribes optimism and freedom from stress.

Pride of place has also been given to Zen-style sculptures of the 18 verses, in pure black granite rock, billions of years old, from near the ancient city of Hampi.

Ajay Piramal is in a nostalgic mood and talks passionately about how he diversified from textiles to a totally unrelated area like pharmaceuticals.

"Manufacturing is finite but human intellect is infinite. Textile is all about manufacturing and industries like pharmaceuticals are all about human intellect," he says.

In 1988, he heard from a friend that Nicholas Laboratories, an Australian MNC that was exiting India, was up for sale. There were many large suitors but Piramal decided to meet Mike Barker, the man in charge of selling the company. He told him that he had no track record, was only 33, but was confident of achieving his dream of putting Nicholas among the top five Pharma companies in India. (It was in the 48th place at that time.) Barker laughed with disbelief but decided to sell the company to him after hearing the **'young and untried entrepreneur's'** turnaround plan.

Piramal says proudly that a decade later, he went to see Barker in retirement in Kenya. He took with him the Nicholas' annual report which showed that the company was among the top five Pharma companies in India through a string of overseas acquisitions like the Indian subsidiaries of Roche, Boehringer Mannheim, Rhone Poulenc, ICI and Hoechst Research Centre. The tradition continues till date as Nicholas sealed two acquisitions over the last two months and is looking out for more.

He is also immensely proud of **Crossroads**, India's first shopping mall. The company had a large factory in the centre of Mumbai and if he wanted to expand, civic permission would be impossible to get. Moreover, the cost of manufacturing was one of the highest in India. The three factory buildings of the pharmaceutical company were converted into retail space with the help of architects from Singapore. On the opening day, cars lined up for miles and the McDonald's ice-cream shop in the mall sold more cones in a day at the Crossroads than in any other store in Asia.

We are through with the rather sumptuous lunch, and Piramal says his father had taught him an important lesson - being with animals teaches you to have respect for all living things. His love for horses (Daffodil, a pure white filly, is his favourite) is hereditary and Piramal remembers his father's *haveli* in Bager, Rajasthan.

There were two ways to enter the house, one a staircase and the other a ramp which was made so that a horse could go with its master to his bedroom. As we walk down the corridor to the lift, he also remembers a blind cheetah on the South African savannah. She was blinded in one eye by a snake but could still hunt and protect her cubs, and didn't let her disability turn her into a useless creature. **"Disabilities and misfortune can make you stronger,"** Piramal says.

sources:http://www.rediff.com/money/2005/nov/08lunch.htm

His strategy of acquiring cheap assets and selling at high valuations may not have impressed shareholders, but after the mega deal with Vodafone, peers are quick to compare him with the Oracle of Omaha.

'Buy cheap and sell high' is a simple investment principle first taught by Ben Graham and David Dodd at Columbia School way back in 1928, but few have followed it with the discipline of Warren Buffett.

The world's second-richest man, the Chairman of Berkshire Hathaway, built his empire by putting the principle at the centre of all his investments. Few others have met with similar success, but, of late, the corporate world is abuzz with the rise of India's own value investor, Ajay Piramal, chairman of the Piramal group. He too has made a career out of buying cheap assets and selling them at a high value.

Many would say it is audacious to call Piramal the Buffett of India because he's just been in the right place at the right time. That might be true, but there's no denying that his business strategy has been driven by value and not vanity. Several Indian businessmen, including some very distinguished ones, are paying a price for their extravagant acquisitions made during the boom years. Piramal stayed away from those even if he was tempted for a while. If nothing else, then just for sticking to the principle of value investing, Piramal deserves credit.

If taking contrarian bets defines value investing, then Piramal has done it all his life. He bought a string of pharmaceutical companies when large multinationals were selling them cheap in the 1980s. He made acquisitions abroad when the Indian currency was at its strongest and stayed away from popular sectors (infrastructure and real estate) that other Indian businesses were chasing mindlessly between 2007 and 2010. He risked his credibility by selling a successful business to Abbott when the world was queuing up to get a foothold in India.

The jury may still be out on Piramal's new businesses and where they are headed, but he has demonstrated that he can generate superior returns even in these market conditions. Merchant banker Vallabh Bhansali considers Piramal unique because he can acquire businesses, build businesses from scratch and sell them when the time is right. "Over the years, he has often asked me why investors have not given a fair value to his businesses, but today I don't think he is waiting for India to understand him," says Bhansali.

On the other hand, Amit Tandon of Institutional Advisory Services maintains that investors of Piramal Enterprises, the group flagship, had put their money in a healthcare company. And if the company chose not to remain in that business, it should have returned the cash.

Indeed, the investors of Piramal Enterprises are not amused as the company's consolidated earnings per share (EPS) went into negative territory: Rs. 13.2 in 2012-13 from Rs. 21.4 in 2009-10 (this was prior to the sale of its domestic formulations business to Abbott for $3.72 billion). The company had a market capitalization of Rs. 10,107 crore, up 16% from Rs. 8,668 crore on 21st May, 2010, a day before it sold the domestic formulation business. SENSEX, the benchmark index of BSE closed at 22,461, up 36.5% from 16,445 on 21st May.

Sitting on a pile of cash

By selling the domestic formulations business, the company divested its most profitable operational business, but did not distribute the money earned as it believed in building new businesses. While that takes time, high amount of cash on the books has dragged the return on capital employed (ROCE) to 2.51% in 2012 - 2013 from 24.23% in 2009 - 2010. Hence, Piramal Enterprises needs to look for investment opportunities till its operational businesses gain scale and require cash to give better returns.

"The board has identified four broad businesses that it will have a presence in - pharmaceuticals (both domestic and international), infrastructure, financial services and the information business (Decision Resources Group) - which will not give results overnight," says Deepak Satwalekar, an independent director on the board of Piramal Enterprises. "We resisted the pressure to invest in haste. The Vodafone deal came up at that time.

We knew it was a short-term deal and yet would yield good returns, investment and operational business strategies can both co-exist, but as operational businesses grow, the pool of funds for short-term deployment will shrink."

What makes Piramal unique as an entrepreneur is possibly his ability to spot a trend early and his ability to cash in at the right time without bringing emotion into it. It's for this reason that many in the corporate world have begun to refer to him as the Buffett of India. His critics may not have forgiven him for selling a highly successful business back in 2010, but the valuation he got suggests that the decision wasn't a losing proposition. Piramal sold the branded generics business to Abbott in 2010 for $3.7 billion (Rs. 18,000 crore), which was nine times the sale and 30 times the EBITDA (earnings before income tax depreciation and amortization). Had he not sold, he would have had to grow the business at 20% year-on-year with an operating margin of 35% for the next 20 years to break even at similar levels.

Narayanan Vaghul, former chairman of ICICI Bank and an independent director on the board of Piramal Enterprises, describes Piramal as a successful acquisitionist who uses his ability to manage organizations and talent to his advantage. "I would not call him Buffett. I don't see him emerging as a private equity player, but as someone who will be focused on four or five businesses. What he does next will be driven by what happens in the country."

The other big criticism Piramal faced back then was the utilization of the money he got from Abbott. Three years on, Piramal is laughing all the way to the bank and making headlines for the windfall gains he made by selling his stake in the telecom company to Vodafone. He earned 52% on his investment of Rs. 5,894 crore made two years ago. While some of his peers are beginning to see sense in his style of investing, analysts aren't just yet buying into his philosophy. Questions are still being raised on whether the company should be investing or building businesses.

Piramal's answer never changes, as he says in jest, "I am always consistent as I have said that these opportunities will come but our goal is to create long-term shareholder value by building operational businesses."

Despite his protestations, his style of value investing is getting talked about and compared with that of Buffett. Over the last three years, he has demonstrated his ability to generate superior returns, be it by building a business, selling it or by deploying capital in a dispassionate manner. He started building the pharmaceutical business in 1988 when multinationals were leaving the country as they saw no value in staying on. Piramal recalls that at that time, these companies had great brands and were sitting on valuable physical assets like land. He joined the fire sale and built a pharmaceutical business, straddling different segments.

"We don't see investments the way others do. We take contrarian bets because we see opportunities where others don't."

Similarly, he sold the business when he felt that competing with Big Pharma would be tough in the generics space. "We try to take little more of a contrarian approach, not because of the sake of being contrarian but because we see the opportunity, yet none of this is a result of a set pattern," he says. "*If everyone is doing the same then you cannot make abnormal returns* - that is the rule of economics."

The common thread

Though there is a vast difference in the scale of operations of Piramal Enterprises and that of Berkshire Hathaway, both the companies have significant amount of cash to invest. Piramal does not deny that his style of investments is driven by the same principle that drives Buffett. Both champion the strategy of contrarian bets and believe in having operational companies as well as pure investment plays. At the height of the sub-prime crisis following the collapse of Lehman Brothers in 2008, Berkshire Hathaway invested $5 billion in Goldman Sachs Group. For Buffett, it generated a return of $3.1 billion in 2013.

Then in November 2010, Buffett surprised the markets by buying the remaining 77.4% stake in Burlington Northern Santa Fe Railway for $26 billion. He bought at a time when the industry was seeing one of its toughest times and had a low valuation.

He is now reaping the benefit as the US economy revives. Similarly, in spite of the slowdown in commercial vehicles, Piramal Enterprises bought a 9.9% stake in commercial vehicle financier Shriram Transport Finance for Rs. 1,652 crore in May 2013. It was a strategic bet as the company had huge cash reserves which could be used by Piramal to invest in promising businesses. Piramal is certainly waiting for the revival of commercial vehicle demand to benefit from this investment.

Deepak Parekh, chairman at mortgage lender, HDFC, says, "Piramal has a sharp nose to smell the deal first and then has the ability to decide fast on both buying and selling."

Piramal Enterprises has focused on three business verticals which have garnered revenue of Rs. 3,400 crore in the first nine months of 2013 - 2014 with EBITDA of Rs. 800 crore. More than a third of this revenue, about Rs. 1,200 crore, came from its contract manufacturing business of the pharmaceutical vertical. This vertical contributed another Rs. 790 crore of revenue with its generic anaesthetic products and over-the-counter products.

The last piece of this vertical, the drug discovery business, is still in trial phase with a pipeline of 13 compounds and no revenue.

The company may see its biggest growth in the near future coming from the other two verticals: information management and financial services. In May 2012, Piramal had bought US-based Decision Resources Group which does data analytics for the healthcare industry. This contributed revenue of Rs. 730 crore in the nine-month period. The financial services business comprises a non-banking finance company and a real estate fund. This brought the company revenue of Rs. 560 crore in the nine-month period.

While the company is in the process of building these businesses, Piramal doesn't want to let go of short-term opportunities like Vodafone to make money.

sources:http://www.business-standard.com/article/companies/is-ajay-piramal-the-warren-buffett-of-india-114041501418_1.html

Rakesh Jhunjhunwala's Success Story: From Rs. 5,000 to $1.8 Billion

sources:https://www.google.co.in/search?q=antohny+robbins+pics&biw=13 66&bih=643&tbm=isch&tbo=u&source=univ&sa=X&ved=0CCkQsARq FQoTCIOVmdmxm8gCFVUGjgod-KINxQ#tbm=isch&q=Rakesh+Jhun- jhunwala+pics&imgrc=pbNabt60YYtB4M%3A

Rakesh Jhunjhunwala is the name that needs no introduction. He is the legendary investor who is known as the Warren Buffet of India. Let's check out the success story of Rakesh Jhunjhunwala and his journey from Rs. 5,000 to Rs. 8,000 crore.

Rakesh Jhunjhunwala was born on 5th July, 1960. His father, an income tax officer, was interested in stocks and used to discuss the stock market with his friends. Rakesh Jhunjhunwala, as a child, would listen to them.

Once he asked his father why price fluctuates. His father told him to check the news, that's what makes the price fluctuate. This was his first lesson on the stock market.

He got fascinated by stocks and found it extremely interesting. He expressed to his father, his wish to get into the stock market. His father told him he could do whatever he wanted in life but first, he should get professionally qualified. Rakesh Jhunjhunwala took up Chartered Accountancy and got his CA degree in 1985.

After getting his CA degree, he told his father that he wanted to get into the stock market. His father reacted by telling him not to ask him or any of his friends for money. He must earn and trade with his own money. Rakesh started his career in 1985 when the BSE Sensex was at 150. He made his first big profit of Rs. 0.5 million in 1986 when he sold 5,000 shares of Tata Tea at a price of Rs. 143, which he had purchased for Rs. 43 a share just 3 months ago.

Between 1986 and 1989, he earned Rs. 2.5 million. His first major successful bet was with the iron mining company, Sesa Goa (now known as SesaSterlite). He bought 400,000 shares of Sesa Goa worth Rs. 10 million in forward trading, and sold about 250,000 shares at Rs. 60 – 65, and another 100,000 at Rs. 150 – 175. When the price rose to Rs. 2200, he sold some shares.

Rakesh Jhunjhunwala bought shares worth Rs. 6 crore of Titan in 2002 - 2003 at an average price of around Rs. 3. The stock is currently trading at a level of Rs. 390 and his investment value is now Rs. 2,100 crore, which made for him around Rs. 35 lakh per hour. In 2006, he bought LUPIN shares for around Rs. 150, which is now trading at Rs. 1100. He bought CRISIL at around Rs. 200 – 300, which is now at Rs. 1800. Likewise, there are many more stocks in his portfolio that made huge money for him.

His Philosophy

Rakesh Jhunjhunwala believes in the power of mistakes. He says it's the mistakes that made him learn and become a better investor. He says, "**If you don't believe the markets are supreme, you will never admit that it was your mistake. If you don't admit that it is your mistake, you will never learn. To succeed in the stock market, not only is the ability to learn from one's mistakes vital but also to blame only oneself for it**. I don't blame the promoters of companies, I blame myself. The promoter is what he is. I have to recognize that he is not what I expect him to be."

Rakesh Jhunjhunwala says what he has learned in life is to try and earn money in trading and to invest it in stocks.

His Belief in India

Rakesh Jhunjhunwala says he is bullish about the country's growth since he entered the stock market. He insists the Indian economy will grow by 9 - 10 percent, though that may need a transition of two to three years.

Rakesh Jhunjhunwala's thesis is that Indians will save $1 trillion a year, and even if 10% of that money, i.e. $100 billion, flows into the markets, there will be a tsunami on the bourses. "So I remain bullish that, for the next 20 years, we could see a bull run like the one Wall Street had from 1987."

sources:http://investorji.in/rakesh-jhunjhunwala-success-story.html

As long term investors we should listen to this great mind. So many fundamentally solid stocks are well off their intrinsic values and yet, they seem to find no buyers! After doing a bit of research into whether I was missing something, I found this interview of Rakesh Jhunjhunwala. Apparently, he too shares my confusion. But his claims that this is one of the **best times to buy equities** got me excited and I thought I should share it with you.

The interview dispersed pearls of wisdom, which reiterates the fact that disciplined investing into good fundamental stocks reaps long term benefits for retail investors.

One of the Best Times to Buy Equities:

When the 'Big Bull' speaks, everyone pays rapt attention, and I too was absorbed listening to his keen observations about the stock market, the macros of the economy and his sectoral views, reflecting on the possible causes of pessimism in the emerging markets in general. Low commodity prices and basic structural imbalances (especially in China) were cited as the reasons for growth moderation amidst high expectations.

Referring to the USA as an 'economy on steroids,' he mentioned that the hyped recovery in its economy, as shown by improvement in the housing sector, is not backed by the savings and earnings growth rate, making it less real and less sustainable. Though unemployment rate in US fell to 7.4 percent in first half of 2013, quantitative easing is not expected to end any time soon. However, the quantity of bond purchases might be reduced.

His proclamations about the Indian markets though, were quite optimistic and were validating my line of thought. According to him, the depreciating values of the Rupee, exit of FIIs and low corporate earnings have impacted the stocks without a doubt, but the fact that the Nifty has not cracked the psychological 7000 barrier, is certainly a cause for some cheer. His belief in the macro-economic prospects of the Indian markets remains strong.

He shared his belief that some stocks are receiving ridiculously low valuations, so low that even if uncertain macro-economic conditions are considered, they appear to be *'chori ka maal.'*

Given how far off their intrinsic value these fundamentally strong companies are, it wouldn't be too much to expect a growth of 17 - 18% CAGR from the Indian markets over a period of the next 7 - 8 years. In his view, the Indian retail investors should, in fact, go ahead with investing in the market and pick fundamentally strong stocks for long term at these *'chor bazaar'* rates.

Talking about the potential upside, he said that it is quite possible to get even a 24% CAGR on solid stocks, with the assumption that the macro environment might cause some short term pain to investors.

Sector-specific views:

When asked about his views on specific sectors, Rakesh Jhunjhunwala said that he is extremely optimistic about the pharmaceutical sector for the next 10 years. He also felt that investors need to revise their expectation from the IT sector, since this sector has now matured. Even the Rupee depreciation would not be able to push the returns of this sector beyond 12 - 18%.

Regarding the banking sector, especially PSU banks, he said that investors need to choose their picks carefully, keeping in mind the fundamentals of individual companies. India is a fairly unbanked country. Thus, a huge potential for financial inclusion points towards good growth is expected from the banking sector. And going by the valuations of PSU banks, there is a lot of money to be made on those in the long term as well.

Regarding the current account deficit (CAD) issues India is currently reeling under, all possible measures are being taken to reduce the import of gold. Recent RBI regulations on gold import have therefore impacted Titan Industries.

When asked about his crown jewel, Titan Industries, which forms a decent portion of his portfolio, he shared his optimism about the stock despite the short term pessimism hovering around it. He claimed that while Titan might post low ROCE numbers owing to the high capital employed, the overall ROCE will still remain high. What remains to be seen is whether Titan can pass on its high interest costs onto their customers.

The message from the 'Big Bull' is loud and clear to me. This is hardly a time for **pessimism**. On the contrary, investors should be diving head-on into the stock markets, as from these valuations, there is nowhere to go but up.

The key message is to have a 5-year horizon and be ready for some short term pain. But investing in good stocks at these levels will certainly give solid returns in the long term, provided the investors are willing to assess the risks associated with investing in stocks and pick fundamentally strong stocks.

sourcehttps://in.finance.yahoo.com/news/interesting-interview-rakesh-jhunjhunwala-060410454.html

I was very happy to find that many stocks in my portfolio were the same as in Rakesh Jhunjhunwala's portfolio. This made me proud of my stock identification skills.

Before I conclude this chapter, I would like you people to seriously think on the following ways in which we act, most of the time:

When there are discounts in the market, on certain items in the grocery shop, on certain brands, on gold jewellery or on some general items of daily use, we (not just the middle class but the upper middle class people too) buy and accumulate the discounted items. There is nothing wrong in doing this. I have seen people like to purchase even the things they don't need. The discounts force them to change their mind. On the other hand, we avoid the shops when there are no discounts at all, especially for luxury items. Am I not right?

But when it comes to stock market, people do just the opposite. They take a big U-turn. When there are big discounts in the stock market, that is when the share market falls, people get scared. Because of the **fear psychosis** that sets in, people want to sell. And they definitely don't purchase when the market is down. If the market reverses, that is if it is up, people's **greed** sets in and they invest as if that share market will keep rising and will never come down.

Dear friends, don't do this. It is **not right**. You know, every year, there are one to two big corrections (*of 400 NIFTY points*) and eight to ten or more small corrections (*of 100 NIFTY points*) and many corrections of 50 NIFTY points. You will get **many opportunities** to purchase, so don't worry, you won't miss the bus.

Please look at the trends below and you will understand What am I really trying to say.

On the following dates, the SENSEX index suffered major single-day falls (of 430 or more points):

24 August 2015 - 1,624.51 points
21 January 2008 - 1,408.35 points
24 October 2008 - 1,070.63 points
17 March 2008 - 951.03 points
3 March 2008 - 900.84 points
22 January 2008 - 875 points
6 July 2009 - 869.65 points
6 January 2014 - 855 points
6 January 2015 - 854.86 points
11 February 2008 - 833.98 points
18 May 2006 - 826 points
10 October 2008 - 800.51 points
13 March 2008 - 770.63 points
17 December 2007 - 769.48 points
16 August 2013 - 769.41 points
7 January 2009 - 749.05 points
31 March 2008 - 726.85 points
6 October 2008 - 724.62 points
05 may 2015 - 722 points
17 October 2007 - 717.43 points
15 September 2008 - 710.00 points
22 September 2011 - 704.00 points
18 January 2008 - 687.82 points
21 November 2007 - 678.18 points

26 March 2015 - 654.25 points
3 September 2013 - 651.47 points
16 August 2007 - 642.70 points
17 August 2009 - 626.71 points
2 April 2007 - 617 points
1 August 2007 - 615 points
9 March 2015 - 604.17 points
27 June 2008 - 600.00 points
27 Aug 2013 - 590.05 points
28 April 1992 - 570 points
17 May 2004 - 565 points
24 February 2011 - 545.92 points
16 December 2014 - 538.12 points
20 June 2013 - 526.41 points
8 July 2014 - 517.97 points
30 January 2015 - 498.82 points
9 February 2015 - 490.52 points
27 February 2012 - 477.82 points
15 May 2006 - 463 points
22 May 2006 - 457 points
31 May 2013 - 455.10 points
18 Nov 2013 - 451.32 points
19 May 2006 - 453 points
6 August 2013 - 449.22 points
16 November 2010 - 444.55 points
4 February 2011 - 441.92 points
12 November 2010 - 432 points
13 May 2013 - 430.65 points

Sources: https://en.wikipedia.org/wiki/BSE_SENSEX

People are in the habit of purchasing at high price. If you do the same, you will also **regret**. But then, you can say, "*Sanjay, how can I know when the market is going to fall?*" If the market has been rising for 4 continuous days, then it is going to fall. If NIFTY has been up 500 points in 2 months, then there is a big correction coming. There's no doubt about it!!!

When people are getting greedy and foolish and buying at ridiculous valuations, then please be cautious. Don't put your money. If possible, sell some stocks but sit on cash. When fear sets in the market and everybody is selling, then you must identify stock with cheap valuations and purchase some, but don't invest 100% cash in the stock market. I generally put in 25% of my cash if NIFTY corrects by 400 points or more in a day.

I have seen people purchase high valued stocks on an impulse, without doing any investigation. I say to them, "**Are you going to die tomorrow or is the share market(BSE/NSE) going to windup business from tomorrow?**" The share market is going to stay for the next 30 years and I hope you are going to live for that long. Then why are you getting into a panic and purchasing without doing proper investigation? Please give this a thought. It is important to understand.

Unlimited wealth will flow if you understand this strategy.

GOD BLESS YOU.

CHAPTER 9

BIRDS OF A FEATHER FLOCK TOGETHER

*H*ave you ever heard the phrase, "Birds of a feather flock together"? If you've ever watched birds in nature, you will know that this phrase holds true. If you look at a flock of birds, you will notice it's made up of the same kind of birds.

For example, you might see a group of sparrows flying together.

You usually won't see a sparrow, a seagull, a buzzard, a cardinal and a crow flying together. That sure would be a sight, though, wouldn't it?

So why do birds flock together? Scientists believe that birds tend to fly and hang out together in flocks because there's safety in numbers.

Flocking together helps birds stay safe from predators.

One bird alone might be easy for a predator, such as a cat, to attack. However, a cat wouldn't stand much of a chance against a flock of ten or more birds.

Did you know that people sometimes behave the same way? It's true! "Birds of a feather flock together," is an old proverb that is often used to describe groups of people.

A proverb is an old saying that's considered wise or good advice. "Birds of a feather flock together," has been around in the English language since the mid-1500s.

When applied to people, this phrase means that people who are similar to each other or share similar interests tend to spend time with each other. You've probably noticed this at school. The friends you used to hang out with were probably people who were similar to you or who liked the same things as you did.

It's only natural for people with similar interests to hang out together. However, it doesn't mean that you always have to spend time with the same people. People have many different interests, so you may be part of many different groups that share different interests.

For example, if you play soccer, you may hang out with your soccer teammates from time to time, but you might also love to play chess, which means you might also hang out with friends who are on the chess team.

Sources:http://wonderopolis.org/wonder/do-birds-of-a-feather-flock-together/

This is the main reason that kept me small. If I was driven by poverty thoughts, how could I be rich? Some 20 years ago, I was completely driven by poverty thoughts and doubts on everything I did. It meant that I was living a life of low self esteem and lack of confidence. Anyway, my brother Naresh Gupta (People knew him as Bobby. He is no more.) We used to have a small grocery store beside our house where we lived. I had a share trading account with him and we had some 50 shares of the State Bank of India, which was trading at Rs. 250. So, we decided to sell and invest the same amount on the shares of another company. In those days we had to do a lot of things manually and we had to depend completely on brokers to sell or purchase shares. Also, we had to send the physical shares to the registrar to get them transferred to our names. So, things were quite different from what they are today and we had to wait for months to get the shares transferred.

We got some Rs. 12,000 from our selling proceeds and invested the entire amount on what the broker has suggested - on some share that was trading at Rs. 11. Few years later, I discovered that the same stock no longer appeared in the newspaper. So, I called the broker about this company and his words shocked me. I want to quote what he said verbatim:

Broker: This stock was last traded at Rs. 2. If you wish, I can enquire more about this company.

Me: Okay, please do so immediately.

A few days later, he called.

Broker: This stock is trading at Rs. 1.50. What do you want to do?

Me: Sell immediately.

Later...

Broker: Your stocks sold at Rs 1.45 per share. We will pay you the money once we receive it.

Me: Okay.

But he did not pay. Months passed and finally I had to recover the money from him. I had a good stock (SBI), but purchased these stupid shares and made a heavy loss. I was not even able to get 25% of the original amount paid in the SBI issue. **Why** did this happened? It is because I always associated with people who had similar poverty thoughts. Also the broker was poor and lived in a poor house and drove an old scooter.

I will give you another example.

I worked at an IT job with a company called Churchill in 1999. I used to travel by chartered bus from Nehru Place, New Delhi to Meerut, though my office was at Greater Kailash, New Delhi.

I used to travel with a friend, who worked in Nehru Place for a brokerage house. I always loved investing and stocks fascinated me. One company looked promising, so I asked my friend to purchase that company's shares for Rs. 50,000 through his brokerage house. (This was the money I had in my savings account with ANZ Grindlays Bank, now called Standard Chartered Bank.)

Again, you can relate this example to the proverb "Birds of a feather flock together."

I was able to acquire this stock at Rs. 46 (approx. $0.7 USD). But a few months later, my friend said, "As you need money for your marriage, why don't you sell this stock? Also, I have inside information that the share market is going to crash in a few months." (He was a very nice man and the stock market did crash.) As the stock was trading at Rs. 57 at that time, I decided to sell. Now this stock is trading at **Rs 1,780** (approx. $26.5 USD). I had poverty thoughts, not rich thoughts, so I liked similar people. You can't be rich with poverty thoughts. Your subconscious mind will keep you poor.

> **"Think Big no matter what."**
>
> — *Sanjay*

Let me tell you, getting rich is not going to be easy. It will be difficult. You will experience a lot of setbacks, disappointments, a whole lot of pain, and a lot of people will leave you. Even better, that you leave a lot of people.

People will call you with lot of names - mad (*pagal*), crazy, insane, idiot, fool. People don't wish you ill but they don't want you to leave them. So, they will try to give suggestions - based on their limited knowledge and understanding.

But, if you really want to get rich, stop flocking with them immediately. If your relationship is getting abusive, then there is no point in sticking to it. Respect is both- sided. You should stop respecting those people who are in the habit of abusing you.

> **"Garbage in, garbage out"**
>
> — *Sanjay*

If you keep hanging out with the same old people, how can new people come into your life? If you keep maintaining your old portfolio, then how will you have a new one?

If your mind is filled with old, limiting beliefs and negative thoughts like "I am not good enough," then how can you have blissful, happy, winning, opulent thoughts?

In a lot of old Hindi movies, we see that to maintain love and peace a man doesn't speak up at all while a woman with ill intentions does all kinds of unhealthy things/tricks and manipulates people/facts with untrue statements. This goes on for 40 - 50 years, till one day, this man takes a stand and says enough is enough, and that he won't tolerate this nonsense. That is when things change. And the film ends with a happy family. So why don't we take the stand now? Why wait for 40 - 50 years to be happy? Decide to hang around with positive people and stop flocking with negative, critical, complaining people.

You need to understand your habit of flocking with failures - people who don't have dreams and goals. You must replace them with those who are dreamers and achievers, people with passion, love and a positive outlook to life who keep working on their dreams and goals.

This is the main reason why people do not grow. They blame circumstances for not being able to achieve their goals and dreams. They often say that other people are responsible for their failure. The truth is that you and only you are responsible for your failures. People do what is good for them. If it is not good for you, then please stop flocking with them, leave them. They don't deserve your love and respect. You need to be very clear on this.

GOD BLESS YOU.

CHAPTER 10

GRATITUDE

Feeling gratitude and not expressing it is like wrapping a present and not giving it.
— *William Arthur Ward*

When I was a kid my father used to say, "We would have been very rich if I had been able to start a bread factory for which I needed Rs. 7,000, which was denied to me at the last moment." I don't want to go into details, but all this depends on the vibration you are sending to the universe. Are we sending positive vibes or negative vibes for others?

If we are thinking positive thoughts about others and helping them achieve their goals and dreams (you don't have to invest your money or time for this, just two minutes of daily prayers will do), how is it possible that your goals and dreams are not fulfilled? The universe never leaves anything in vacuum.

It works like magic. Please do it. The theory behind this is - if you are not grateful to the universe (God or the supreme power) for the things you already have (that were given to you by the universe), then what is the guarantee that you will be grateful to the universe for your future goals and dreams?

The following lines should be repeated ten times in the morning after waking up and ten times in the evening before going to bed.

"I AM SO HAPPY AND GRATEFUL FOR EVERY LITTLE THING THAT MY LIFE HAS BEEN BLESSED WITH."

— *Sanjay*

You need to understand that "As we sow, so shall we reap." People are not clear about their dreams and goals (their own, not those of their parents, partners or friends). I think most of you have seen the movie '3 Idiots.'

In the film, from the day Farhan Qureshi was born, his father proclaimed that he would get an engineer. But when he got admission into an engineering college, he realised that being an engineer was never his dream. It was his father's dream. Out of love and respect, he tried to fulfil what his father wanted for him, even though it was not what he himself wanted. He pursued engineering only to please his father and make him happy.

He had a passion for photography and his dream was to become a wildlife photographer.

Aren't most people doing the same thing? People who see the film criticize the father, whereas at home they behave the same way. People not only choose what they love to do in their own lives, but choose for you as well. If this is a rule, then you should have the right to choose for their lives as well. So, follow your dreams, not those of your parents, partners or friends.

My wife loves her job so much that she can't think of leaving it or retiring. She has great passion for her work. I, on the other hand, don't have the same passion for a job. My passion lies in stocks, mutual funds, and motivating people to come out of their financial mess.

People always want to dominate and control you. You can't imagine how they control you and make you to obey their orders. If you are smart and refuse to obey their orders, they play emotional games with you. And the emotional games and tricks they use can get very dirty and painful. Ultimately you are left with no choice but to fulfil their ill wishes and greedy choices.

If you revert back even with 10% of what they said to you, then they will refuse to listen and shout at you. They say, "You accepted this decision, you were happy about it. If things are bad now, you can't blame us." Well, if things were that good and every decision was according to my desire, then why I was living a depressed life and having suicidal thoughts till 2008? To stop these noises from interfering with your life, tell these guys to SHUT UP! Respect is earned, not demanded. Even if they are older than you, then also you can have a choice and say **NO** to them.

It is all in the vibrations that you are sending out to the universe. You can't fool the universe. The **TRUTH** will not change if you deny it. **Don't live your life trying to fulfil other people's goals and dreams**.

You love your family and friends and do many things out of respect for them. They too need to understand their boundaries in the relationship. If the relationship is getting abusive, you must leave it. There is no point in sticking on to an unhealthy relationship.

I call such people extra-smart people. They are everywhere. You don't need special eyes to find them.

Remember the following words and repeat them to yourself everyday:

Ask, and it will be given to you.
Seek, and you will find.
Knock, and it will be opened for you.

I would like to thank self-help books and videos, including the wonderful video by T.S. Madaan.

My intention was never to hurt anybody. Over the years I have never shared my feelings, frustrations, anger and anguish with anybody. Only Garima knows a little about them (and she is not interested in talking about my past life). Usually, there are 3 types of people.

1. Winners
2. Losers
3. And people who don't know how to win

I have gone through all the 3 stages, and in the process I discovered how to **WIN**. Now I clearly know what should be done to win and how it feels to be a **WINNER**. I understand the power of good stocks and SIP.

I have discovered how to live a blissful **HAPPY** life. And the power of a great investment portfolio. Therefore, through this book, I am sharing some of my experiences and feelings on this subject.

sources:https://www.google.co.in/search?q=antohny+robbins+pics&biw=136 6&bih=643&tbm=isch&tbo=u&source=univ&sa=X&ved=0CCkQsARqF QoTCIOVmdmxm8gCFVUGjgod-KINxQ#tbm=isch&q=POWER+POISI- NG+pics&imgrc=SewvNawOBKTPcM%3A

You need to do **POWER POSING**. It is a very powerful thing. I do it a lot and have achieved the impossible with it. I am not asking you to do this in front of everybody, or in the interview room, or on a negotiation table when you are about to sign a big deal.

But you can go inside a washroom, where nobody is watching you, stand there in power pose for **TWO MINUTES**. Close your eyes and visualize yourself achieving success in whatever you are there for. And say to yourself, "Yes, I did it." You need not say this loudly. You can say it quietly to yourself. Don't bother if you fail in the interview or aren't able to get that deal through. You will not get results immediately. But keep doing it, and believe in the power of posing. Folks, what happens is that: Power posing raises testosterone levels and lowers the stress hormone called cortisol. That's not all. Something bigger happens at the subconscious level and after some time, your subconscious mind starts believing that you can do it! It starts creating circumstances to make it possible. And wonderful things begin to happen. I will share more on the power of the subconscious mind in my motivational books. I learned about this a few years ago from Amy Cuddy, TED Talks.

Let me give you an example from my own life. I watch the film, 'Law of Attraction' quite often. I have watched it more than 50 times already. A few years ago, I started losing my hair. It grew more and more thin every day. I tried many hair creams, hair oils, popped tablets and wasted more than Rs. 50,000 (approx. $750 USD) to stop my hair from falling, and to grow it back. But nothing helped. The more I worried, the more the hair loss. I got really anxious. A lot of balding people feel the same way. Though my hair had not fallen so much that I looked bald, patches of baldness could be noticed on my head.

One night, year ago, I had a nightmare that I was completely bald, with not a strand of hair on my head. I was in a party where there were some friends from a company I previously worked for. One of them said, "Sanjay, four years ago, when we used to work together, you looked so good. Now you are bald!" He began to make fun of me. I noticed some other friends also laughing at me. This was too much for me to handle. I left the party. When I was taking my car out through the driveway, my wife said to me, "Why did you ruin our evening? They were just kidding. If you are bald, accept it. There is nothing wrong in accepting facts." I woke up from my nightmare and looked at the clock. It was 2 am and a cold winter night. I touched my head and looked at myself in the mirror. I still had hair. I was happy.

That night, I decided to do something about my problem. I watched many YouTube videos, searched through many Google pages, read many articles and websites, but nothing was convincing. Then, around 5 am in the morning, a thought struck my mind. If the Law of Attraction is so powerful and works for those who **BELIEVE**, it should work for me if I visualize myself with hair like Hrithik Roshan, the actor. (I love to have hair and a body like his).

From that day onwards, I started to visualize myself with hair like Hrithik Roshan's. Every morning and evening, I would stand before the mirror and say to myself, "Sanjay, you look pretty good. You have hair like Hrithik Roshan's. Jhakaas!" (*Jhakas* means superb. It is a word made popular by the actor Anil Kapoor.) I did this exercise daily, after waking up in the morning and before going to bed.

The next time I went to a salon for a haircut, I asked the barber, "Can you see any new hair growing on my head?" "No," he replied. It was the same answer for 8 months, but I was not ready to quit. I kept on with the exercise. And asked the barber the same question every time I went for a hair-cut. A few months ago, when I visited the salon, my barber finally said, "Sir, there is a little new hair growing. I can see your bald patches getting covered!" Hearing this, I was overjoyed and immediately thanked God.

A few months later, I visited my father in Meerut. He said, "Sanju, I notice you have some new hair growing." To this I replied, "Thank you, Papa. It happened because of positive thinking." I finally got an acknowledgement from my father. That was what I wanted. Once again, I thanked God.

To give power to your goals and dreams, you need to envision things. With your mind's eye, you need to see, and believe in the things which others can't see or believe in. People believe only what they see. If they can't, they will discourage you and give you reasons why it is not possible. Why listen to negative words and get discouraged?

Give credit to people only when it is due. In the year 2008, when I was going through the worst part of my life and it was getting difficult for me to handle life's turmoil, I was living with the idea that nothing was good in me. That nobody liked me. People had wronged me, tricked me and played with my emotions. My past was haunting me and I began to feel suicidal. I would visualize how my previous bosses had humiliated me. One had said, "What I have seen in you that made me, hire you?" I remembered another time, when I was sitting with my boss for my review. To show his power and arrogance, he put both his both legs up on my chair. That was the worst day of my life. I was so humiliated that not only did I decide to quit my job (where I was considered a complete nobody) but to end my life as well.

I will take this opportunity to say a few words to that gentleman - maybe you have achieved great things in the US, or you are considered a God in the company you work for. But remember, you are NOT GOD. The universe never leaves anything in vacuum. If the same things happen to your son someday, and he too is humiliated in the same way as you humiliated others, how will you feel? I have already forgiven you, but remember **God** will not. Someday, you will have to pay the price for your sins.

I couldn't visualize my daughter in tears, growing up hating her father, thinking of me as a coward. so I was not okay to take that dirty step (to end my life), actually I was not being able to get solutions to the problems in my life quickly. a year later, I came across a YouTube video on the life of Gautama Buddha. I became deeply interested in the words of Buddha and felt inspired by his search for the truth. I had finally got the answers I was looking for. I was not at **peace**, so I decided to do something that would help others. I started contributing to UNICEF, then SAVE THE CHILDREN, then HABITAT. But I was not contributing with discipline. Some months, I'd contribute a lot and some months, I'd contribute nothing. But in August 2014, when Narendra Modi became India's Prime Minister, I decided to contribute 1% of my earnings to the PM relief fund, every month, without a break.

Also, I have made a commitment to myself that I will give 5% of whatever I earn from my company or as royalties from my books to the PM relief fund.

"THE SECRET OF HAPPY LIVING IS GIVING"

— Sanjay

I am not asking you to contribute to the PM relief fund. But give something to the poor, through any charity you like. Actually, I want to contribute to the poor people, but find it difficult to trust any charity. There are so many fraudulent trusts operating all around, and I don't have the time to investigate them. That is why I decided to contribute to the PM relief fund. Some may say that there is cheating at that level too. If you think that way then there is a big problem with you. If you doubt everybody, then you can't start contributing, and can never help anyone in your life. I have seen a lot of people, who have a **trust deficit issue**.

Many say, "I contribute by donating my old clothes." That is good, but you are just cleaning out your wardrobe. So, start with small contributions. Help the poor, people who are not as privileged as you. There is no rule that you have to start with 1%. You can even start with 0.1%. Just make sure you do it! Please do not procrastinate this.

I have many stocks in my portfolio which I have purchased at the lowest point of the day, or sold at higher points of the day, and never touched that height again.

If you start by contributing even 1% of your profits to poor, what will happen is that this 1% will apply its force on the universe and you will end up with more profits.

So, generate in yourself **"The Joy Of Giving." It is the ultimate secret.**

In August - September 2015, Indian markets went through a large correction due to the China factor. My portfolio lost 30% of its value from its high. As a result, I churned a lot of shares and purchased some really good quality stock, but the market kept going down. My quality stocks also went down. I said to myself, "Sanjay, hold on. You are not giving properly." So, I quickly made a contribution to the PM relief fund. The next morning, I saw some poor children walking on the streets. I gave them some money and to other groups of children. Today, on the 12th of September 2015, as I write this, my portfolio has already recovered 10% of its value from its low. What has changed?

I can't explain how it works, but it works amazingly well. No cheating is allowed as you cannot cheat the universe and your subconscious mind records everything that you are doing.

I made bigger profits when I tied my returns with these activities.

In the previous chapters, I have already told you how to do disciplined investments. But this is the ultimate secret. It will bring you more happiness and joy than you can imagine. You will have more riches. Just do this and you can enjoy all the luxuries that you have imagined.

You know, if I have to list the names of the people who have wronged me, the list will contain less than 10 names. (I don't hate them. I have already forgiven them, though I still do not like what they did.) But if I list the names of people who have helped me, the list will contain hundreds if not thousands of names. You need to find something to appreciate each day. Develop a habit of looking for good in others. If you notice that people are not smiling, it means that you too are not smiling. Smile and they will smile back.

There was a time when I did not have a chronograph watch. I would dream of owning a Tissot watch, and was planning to buy one. At that time, my bro-in-law, Saurabh, bought me a Swatch watch from Switzerland. Though I had visualized a white coloured dial, it has a dial whose colour was similar to the BMW logo. So, I told him, "This is great. Now I'll have to buy a BMW to match this." Thank you, Saurabh, for the lovely watch you bought for me.

You need to give people the credit due to them. Say thank you often. Respect people. And don't judge people by their status. Give respect and love freely. If you can't say something good about something or somebody then don't say anything at all. Keep your mouth shut. Don't say anything bad about anybody. (Stop yourself from offloading dirt from your mind onto others.)

"FORGIVE PEOPLE WHO HAVE WRONGED YOU."

— *Sanjay*

Forgive. Forgiving means that you have to forgive people who have wronged you, caused you pain, or broken your trust. However, you should not forget the lessons that the experience taught you. These are important lessons that life has taught you, so be sure to remember them. Life is too short to live with the pain they caused.

Forgive anyone who has caused you pain or harm. Keep in mind that forgiving is not for others. It is for you. Forgiving is not forgetting. It is remembering without anger. It frees your power, heals your body, mind and spirit. Forgiveness opens up a pathway to a new place of peace where you can persist despite what has happened to you.

Forgive yourself and create a place of freedom, inner strength and serenity within you. Affirm to yourself - I am now free. Peace, love, and harmony are within and around me. You have something special. You have GREATNESS within you!

— *Les Brown*

You might ask, "Sanjay, if you are so rich why are you not living in a villa or why don't you drive a XUV?"

Folks, I was greatly influenced by Robert Kiyosaki's book, 'Rich Dad Poor Dad.' One important message that is still clear in my mind is, '**Accumulate Assets not Liabilities.**' House and car are liabilities (though middle class people consider them assets). People don't know the difference between assets and liabilities, and *accumulate liabilities thinking that they are assets*. If your house is not generating an income for you, then it is a liability. Only if your house is for rent can then only it be considered an asset. So, Pankaj's (who lives in Pune) house is an asset and mine is a liability.

Secondly, Kiyosaki suggested that you can accumulate liability if you have a supporting income for it. It means that you should not buy a liability by selling assets. So, I don't want to sell my assets to accumulate liability. Also my assets haven't grown to such size that I can buy liability, and I don't want to accumulate liability with a bank loan, where I will end up paying for liability with asset income. You know, I have gone many times with my wife and property brokers to purchase villas/apartments. But I have always backed out from the deal with some excuse or other. Now, it seems the whole world has come to know the truth, including my wife, but that's okay. Also, I have some good neighbours whom I don't want to move away from, because I would miss them too much. :)

People may say, "Everything is good, but POWER POSING should not be part of the chapter on Gratitude." I also thought so initially. Then, I decided to place power posing in the Gratitude chapter because if you can't love and respect yourself, how can you love and respect others?

GOD BLESS YOU.

CHAPTER 11

CONCLUSION

God gave you a gift of 86400 seconds today. Have you used one to say thank you?

— *William Arthur Ward*

More profits will come to you if you do the following things, apart from doing the other things mentioned in other chapters.

Generate a habit of selling stocks within 15 minutes after market opens, i.e. between 9:15 - 9:30 am. And purchase within 15 minutes after 3 pm, i.e. between 3:00 pm to 3:15 pm. If you figure out that the stock you want to purchase is up 5 - 8 percent, then don't purchase on that day. The next day, you will get it at cheaper rates. The above strategy is a good one to follow. 60 – 70 percent of the times, it has worked for me. I have been following this with discipline since 2012.

*NOTE: Try to do most of the transactions using **VTC**. As explained earlier, if VTC order is not executed and you want sell/purchase, do it at market rate. Don't place the order and wait for it to get executed. Most of the time, your order is not executed in 15 minutes with bids.*

I often say, "*India mein free ki advice bahut milti hai.*" That means – "***In India, you can get lot of advice for free.***" If you ask even a beggar on the street about how to live happy and joyful, he will advise you about an infinite number of ways to be so. But is he doing any of the things he is advising? Of course not! These free advisers are available everywhere and they can advise on any topic, without having any knowledge about it.

You know, these advisors have done more damage in my life than you can imagine. And such people seemed to be extremely active around 1998 – 2008. These stupid people don't know anything but are among the first to advice. In 2006 I purchased 1000 units of a share at Rs. 76 per unit of a stock, based on my study of the market. But in 2008, an advisor on a news channel I was watching said that this stock was likely to go down to Rs. 23 anytime soon. I began to doubt every decision I had made and trusted everybody's intelligence but mine. So, I sold all 1000 units at the rate of Rs. 31, with a loss of Rs. 45 per unit. After a few days, this stock went down to Rs 26. It made me feel good and I thought of how intelligent the advisor was. Last year (2014), while I was watching a business channel, this stock came under discussion. Another advisor was saying - the stock in question had gone up too fast, too quickly, and it had a potential to cross Rs. 1000 in a few months. I was stunned and rushed to open my ICICI direct a/c to confirm. My fear was true. The stock was trading at Rs. 800.

Another example, two years ago, somebody advised me to purchase a share which was trading at Rs. 450 then, and said it could go up to Rs. 700 in a few months. I generally, purchase 500 units now this stock is trading at Rs 57, i.e. it has lost about 85 percent of its value. (All I can say to these advisors is, "***Son, I am the principal of the school you study in.***")

Most of the time, these advisors are not correct. They provide nonsense as advice. Doubt them, not yourself. You have greatness in you. You just need to discover it.

Most of these advisors who are ready to advise on any topic drive old cars, live in old houses and have spoilt kids. They are not happy in office or in life, are not able to manage their finances and are always complaining about the government or the economy. Look friends, it is 2015 not 2008, and the worst is over for me. But if you don't change your habit of advising when it is not asked for, I will throw you out of my life. You will find your name on the top of the list of people I don't like. And you can't change my mind even 0.0000001% with your advice. Anyway, if your name is not on the list of people mentioned below, please don't advise me on anything. I don't care how good you think your advice might be.

Narendra Modi (PM of India)

Tony Robbins

Les Brown

Dr. Subhash Chandra

T.S. Madaan

Sandeep Maheshwari

Amy Cuddy

Nick Vujicic

Rakesh Jhunjhunwala

Ajay Piramal

Ajay Bagga (executive Chairman, OPC Asset Solutions)

Udayan Mukherjee (of CNBC-TV18)

Rajat Sharma (chairman and editor in chief of India TV)

Chetan Bhagat(author, columnist, screenwriter, television personality)

Dinish Saini (my friend)

Himani Nargotra(my friend)
Priti Padhy(ex-boss)
Mouad Tiyal(ex-boss)
Abdeslam Alaoui Smaili(HPS director)
Vikas Nagpal(ex-boss)
Mrutunjay Pattanayak(ex-boss)

Now, I am living the life of my dreams and I am financially free, not dependant on a job anymore. All this happened when I stopped listening to the advice of unsuccessful people who don't have goals and dreams in their own lives, and replaced it with advice from the above mentioned guys. If I can do it, so can you. You just need to discover your hidden talent and stop listening to this noise. **God has made you to fulfil your own dreams, not those of your family, friends, relatives etc. Don't spend your life doing things that they would love you to do. You have greatness in you. Discover it and do the things that make you HAPPY. Live your life, challenge the impossible.**

My humble request to CNBC-TV18, ZEE Business, other business channels, and print media that publish business articles - please provide the performance data of your advisors, i.e. the **Hit/Miss** percentage of advisors, if not every month, at least quarterly. This way, investors can know who provides good advice and whose advice is to be ignored.

You will remember that in many parts of this book, I have asked you to increase your **KNOWLEDGE**. I was able to get the financial freedom I desired because I kept on increasing my knowledge of investing. I have not acquired great knowledge in a few days or a few months, but it was over years that I became very good at picking stocks. That is why I'm asking you to increase your knowledge. The more knowledge you have, the more you will GROW. Your confidence will increase and that will translate into **wealth** and the **opulent** life you deserve.

You must say to yourself that, "If I am going through a tough time, financially or mentally, it is because I am reaping what I sowed. So, next time, I will SOW more carefully".

I want you to focus on the following 5 points. Whenever you doubt yourself, please refer to them. They will enable you to take responsibility of whatever you do (most people don't want to take responsibility and are ready with the blame game).

1. **Think:** We need to understand 'what exactly we think about.' We need to know that '*As we sow, so shall we reap.*'

    - We need to be positive in our thinking and avoid all negative thoughts.

    - We need to understand, literally and emotionally, the principle that we become what we think.

2. **Imagination**: Cutting out all negative thoughts from our minds, we need to understand that all limitations are self-imposed. The opportunities offered today and tomorrow are enormous beyond belief.

3. **Courage:** With all courage and energy, think positively about your own problems. Let your mind be open to think about your goals and dreams.

   - Let your mind imagine all possible ways to achieve your goals.
   - Let your mind refuse to believe that there are any circumstances sufficiently strong to defeat the achievement of your goals.
   - Act positively and decidedly towards your goals.

4. **Important:** Save 10% of what you earn and donate 1% of your earnings to any charitable activities that you love.

   - You need to tell your mind, "There are many possibilities for rising in my current work or task, if I am willing to pay the price."

5. **Action:** Ideas are of no use until we act on them.

I shall conclude this book with the following beautiful words:

"**We think luxury can never be defined... it can only be felt. In a way it's like art, if you understand it then you really know it's worth...**"

— *Priyanka Tiku Tripathi (vice-president, marketing,* **FORBES** *INDIA and CNBC-tv18)*

Golden strategy that always works:

1. Stay out of the market when in doubt about market, you don't have to buy/sell stocks daily, long term wealth is created with staying invested for long term, develop patience.

2. Buy on rumours, sell on news, means when you listen rumours about stocks then buy but immediately sell when news is confirmed from reliable source, but this strategy is for traders not for investors.

GOD BLESS YOU.

Happiness comes from doing the things that make you happy. :)

— *Sanjay*

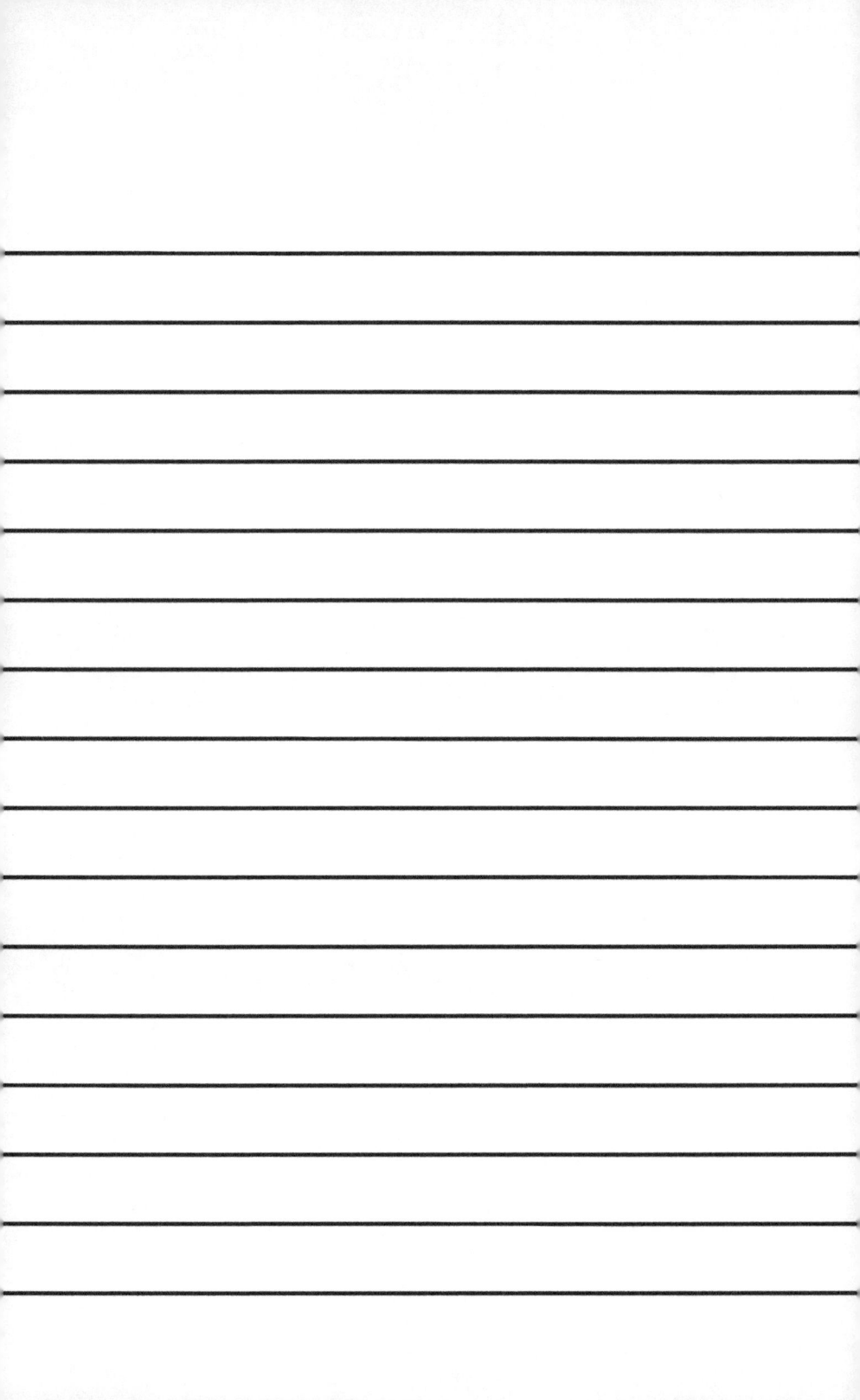

www.ingramcontent.com/pod-product-compliance
Lightning Source LLC
Chambersburg PA
CBHW020425220526
45464CB00002B/570